GENERAL
HOWE'S DOG

GENERAL HOWE'S DOG

——— ✳ ———

George Washington,
the Battle of Germantown,
and the Dog Who Crossed Enemy Lines

Caroline Tiger

Chamberlain Bros.
a member of Penguin Group (USA) Inc.
2005

CHAMBERLAIN BROS.

Published by the Penguin Group

Penguin Group (USA) Inc., 375 Hudson Street, New York, New York 10014, USA

Penguin Group (Canada), 10 Alcorn Avenue, Toronto, Ontario M4V 3B2, Canada
(a division of Pearson Penguin Canada Inc.)

Penguin Books Ltd, 80 Strand, London WC2R 0RL, England

Penguin Ireland, 25 St Stephen's Green, Dublin 2, Ireland
(a division of Penguin Books Ltd)

Penguin Group (Australia), 250 Camberwell Road, Camberwell, Victoria 3124,
Australia (a division of Pearson Australia Group Pty Ltd)

Penguin Books India Pvt Ltd, 11 Community Centre, Panchsheel Park,
New Delhi–110 017, India

Penguin Group (NZ), Cnr Airborne and Rosedale Roads, Albany, Auckland 1310,
New Zealand (a division of Pearson New Zealand Ltd)

Penguin Books (South Africa) (Pty) Ltd, 24 Sturdee Avenue, Rosebank,
Johannesburg 2196, South Africa

Penguin Books Ltd, Registered Offices: 80 Strand, London WC2R 0RL, England

Library of Congress Cataloging-in-Publication Data

Tiger, Caroline.
    General Howe's dog : George Washington, the Battle of Germantown, and
the dog who crossed enemy lines / Caroline Tiger.
        p.   cm.
    Includes bibliographical references.
    ISBN 1-59609-032-4
    1. Germantown, Battle of, Philadelphia, Pa., 1777.   2. Washington,
George, 1732–1799.   3. Howe, William Howe, Viscount, 1729–1814.
    4. Dogs—Pennsylvania—Philadelphia—History—18th century—Miscellanea.
I. Title.

E241.G3T54   2005   2005041423
973.3'33—dc22

Printed in the United States of America
10   9   8   7   6   5   4   3   2   1

Book design by Jaime Putorti

To Mom and Dad,
my earliest teachers
and my most devoted fans

Contents

Introduction

Every October, fighting breaks out on Germantown Avenue in Mt. Airy, a neighborhood about six miles north of the center of Philadelphia. The violence isn't started by a group of rowdy Eagles fans defending their team's honor. No, the hooligans are a group of war reenactors, playing out the battle that, more than two centuries ago, helped turn the tide of the American Revolution. As George Washington's troops did in the wee hours of the morning of October 4, 1777, the reenactors march toward Germantown from the southeast. These modern soldiers are presumably more alert. The eighteenth-century soldiers were operating on raw will and determination. They hadn't slept or eaten much in days. Seventy-pound packs weighed down their skinny frames. Their uniforms were in tatters. The wet ground seeped through their tired, beat-up shoes and into their socks, chilling their sore feet.

As they marched closer and closer to where the British forces were encamped in Germantown, a heavy fog rolled in. Through the mist, the Revolutionaries could just make out crimson flashes of the British—the imperial forces were wearing dapper white trousers, high black boots, and red coats with brass buttons. Their stomachs were full and their attitudes haughty. They awaited Washington's ragtag army. One hundred fifty of them had already taken up position in Cliveden (rhymes with "lived in"), also known as Chew House, the magnificent summer mansion of Benjamin Chew, the Chief Justice of Pennsylvania. With two-foot-thick stone walls, the fortress would be able to withstand musket fire, and the Brits would have a bird's-eye view of their targets.

If you go to Battle of Germantown Day, you'll see the Americans march up Germantown Avenue and up to Cliveden, where their commander decides that they should attack. Honestly, it seems like a mistake from the get-go. (Then again, we do have the advantage of hindsight.) The sad-looking soldiers run past the circular drive and up to the front lawn of the house. They take aim at its windows, where musket tips appear, fire, and quickly disappear. Americans fall wounded on the grass. They charge the house's wooden door and try to pound it in with the ends of their muskets, to no avail. As they retreat, more are shot by window assassins. More Americans fall dead.

It's complete chaos. The muskets are louder than you can imagine, like firecrackers but worse, and they are constant. The smoke from the guns fills the air, and you wonder how the Americans could even hear their commanders' shouts or see where they were firing. They were fighting hungry, sleep-deprived, deaf, and blind. At least seventy-five of them died at Chew House. Overall casualties in the battle broke down to more than eleven hundred losses for the Americans, while the British suffered more than five hundred. (How did this lopsided victory turn the tide in favor of the Americans? You'll have to read on to see.) At the end, the Americans marched the twenty-five miles back to where they'd come from the night before. Still no food. Still no sleep. But they were up one dog. This is the story of that dog.

Somehow, though very little is known about General Howe's dog—as with all unrecorded historical events, much is surmised—his grand adventure has lived on through the last two centuries. The pup has charmed everyone who has come across the account of his escape, capture, and return. His story endures because of what it symbolizes. The tale telegraphs the era's emphasis on gentlemanly conduct, even during a time of war, even during a time of unrestrained violence and detestable atrocities.

There's a huge discrepancy in the information available about the two major players in this particular story. Countless biographies and books have been written on Washington and on the actual battle, but there is scant information about Howe, whose papers all went up in flames in a nineteenth-century house fire. Still, I've attempted to present a complete story here, including an account of the commanders' early years, which led up to the incident. There are also a few chapters to provide context for the era's perspective on dogs and the general view of dogs at war.

Historians have interpreted this tale of General Howe's dog in many different ways. I've tried to present it in a manner that will let you draw your own conclusions. It's fun to conjecture over historic events—after all, the parties involved can't easily argue with you. Would Washington and Howe have been friends if they hadn't been adversaries? Washington was forty-three when he took command of the Revolutionary army. Howe was forty-five when he arrived in America on a mission from the king to quash the Revolutionaries. The two contemporaries came from completely different worlds—one from a farm, the other from a house of nobles—yet they seemed to share more than a few commonalities, including a preference for peace over war, for playing fair, and for card-playing—and a fondness for canines.

✳

Howe and Washington Join the Army

On May 25, 1775, General Sir William Howe sailed into Boston on a British warship, the HMS *Cerberus*. Howe was a soldier with an impressive military career under his belt. He'd been sent by King George III to resolve the conflict that had flared up between England and the colonies.

For more than a decade, colonists had been champing at the bit of British rule. Each time the monarchy attempted to assert tighter control over colonial commerce and government, the colonials resisted by boycotting British goods or refusing to pay the tax. The situation came to a head on an unseasonably warm day in January 1774, when a group of Bostonians posing as Mohawk Indians boarded the *Dartmouth* and threw 342 chests of British tea into Boston Harbor. The tea was worth ten thousand English pounds. Parliament responded strongly. They issued acts that were meant to drive home the message that England was still very much in control of the colonies. They closed the port of Boston. They revoked Massachusetts's charter, announcing that the king would appoint all of the colony's ruling positions from then on. They decreed that royal officials were exempt from being tried in colonial courts, even if they had caused the death of a citizen, meaning there'd be few, if any, repercussions for going after an anti-royal rabble-rouser.

In September, delegates from the twelve colonies came to Philadelphia for the first Continental Congress. There they drafted a petition to the king, a declaration of rights, and an assertion that they would respond force with force should the British troops try to implement these recent acts of Parliament in Massachusetts. King George III did not even consider the possibility of accepting this petition. It was laughable, especially to a man who believed deeply in the system of imperial government. He actually hoped that the rebels would stand by their threat to take on the red-coats, since nothing would convince the colonists of their secondary status like the full force of the British imperial army bearing down upon them.

By all accounts, Howe was not pleased about being sent to Boston. As an English Whig, he believed in the idea of a king at the head of Parliament, but he also sympathized with the Americans' demands for equal rights. As much as he believed in the monarchy, he also believed in the rights of the individual. Of course, William enjoyed extensive individual rights within the empire. As the third and youngest son of a second viscount, he was born into an upwardly mobile aristocratic family. King William III bestowed the title of first viscount upon his paternal grandfather, Scrope Howe. His father, the second viscount, followed in Scrope's footsteps by acting in Parliament, and he was also the royal governor of Barbados for a short time. But the family's prominence was really due to the charms and graces of its women.

William's grandmother Howe was a mistress of

*General William Howe was born to an aristocratic family
that the young George Washington would have envied. By the
time they became adversaries, Washington, like Howe, was
considered every inch the gentleman. Like Washington, Howe
was an avid hunter, and he also had served in the French and
Indian War. Perhaps surprisingly, the men's views on the
American colonies were not as dissimilar as one might suppose.
And while Howe's victories in the New York and Pennsylvania campaigns were celebrated, he was chastised for not following up on these successes. After the war, in 1799, when his
brother Admiral Lord Richard Howe died, he succeeded him as
the fifth Viscount Howe. He had married in 1765, but, like
Washington, had no children. He lived out his life as a country
gentleman, enjoying foxhunting and participating in politics,
and he died on July 12, 1814, in Plymouth, England.*

George I, and the royal family accepted her daughter, Sophia Kielmansegge, as a blood relation. Sophia was believed to be the illegitimate daughter of the king, and she later became the friend and traveling companion of the mistress of George II. As Dowager Countess Howe, Sophia lived in George II's household and received a large annual pension from the crown. The royal family treated her daughter like a cousin. Princess Amelia, George II's daughter, even gave Sophia's daughter a ring bearing the likeness of George I, complete with a crown of diamonds.

Sophia's sons—George, Richard, and William— grew up at court, playing alongside the future King George III. They were schooled at Westminster and Eton, but William, for one, was no great scholar. And since his oldest brother, George, had inherited the title of third viscount, he needed to find some other way to distinguish himself. The obvious choice for him was to join the British army, which he did in 1746, at the age of seventeen.

✳

An ocean away, in 1746, in the English colony of Virginia, a fourteen-year-old named George Washington was wishing he'd been born into the aristocracy. That would have made it much easier for him to fulfill his dream of one day becoming an officer in the British army. Instead, Washington was a fourth-generation American whose family owned a middling plantation enterprise in the Northern Neck region of Virginia. In 1657, Washington's great-grandfather John had made his way to the Americas as first mate on the *Sea Horse*, a ketch following a tobacco route from England to northern Europe and then to Virginia. At each port, John would go ashore to sell tobacco. In Virginia, the ship's mission was to restock, but while she was anchored in the Potomac, the ship got caught in a squall and capsized. By the time she washed up on the shore of the river, she was in need of major repairs. And until the ship was in sailing condition, the crew was stuck in Virginia. Twenty-four-year-old John used his time well. He was taken under the wing of a wealthy Virginian exporter-planter named Nathaniel Pope. A year later, when the ship left for England, Joseph stayed behind and married Nathaniel's daughter, Anne.

George grew up on the ten thousand acres, mostly uncleared, that belonged to Joseph's grandson, Augustine, or "Gus," Washington. The property had a farm with plenty of cows, dogs, pigs, chickens, horses, and tobacco crops. George's mother, Mary Ball, was Gus's second wife; with his first wife, he'd had two sons, Lawrence and Augustine Jr., who were living in England and getting a formal education at the Appleby School. George met them for the first time at age five. Lawrence taught his half brother how to fish, hunt, and ride a horse. But when George was seven, Lawrence left once more. England needed manpower for a war in the Caribbean—the British were trying to seize settlements along valuable trade routes. Red-coated officers rode from town to town in Virginia, recruiting colonists for their cause, and Lawrence applied for and won an officer's commission. His shiny brass facings and spiffy scarlet-and-navy uniform made quite an impression on young George, who made it his mission to one day fight for the British imperial army.

With his brother off at war and his father always away on a quest for more land, George spent most of his time at home with his mother and his younger siblings. He continued to hunt and fish and to explore the wilds of the untamed wilderness around his family's home. He also began his schooling, learning how to

The Fredericksburg, Virginia, home of Mary Ball Washington, the general's mother. George Washington was born in 1732 to a somewhat prosperous Virginia farming family. His father died when he was eleven years old, and Mary, a tough, driven woman, struggled, with the help of her late husband's two sons from a previous marriage, to keep the home together. Young George, with a gift for numbers, combined with quiet confidence and ambition, came to the attention of Lord Fairfax, one of the most prominent men in Virginia. At the age of sixteen, Washington began working for Fairfax as a surveyor. It was during this time that Washington took a fancy to gambling, dancing, theater, and hunting, which became his great passion.

read and write and do arithmetic, first from a tutor and then at a log schoolhouse. He was preparing for his own eventual enrollment in the Appleby School in England.

Unfortunately, the death of George's father when he was eleven years old meant he would never have the opportunity to obtain an English education. There would be no formal training in how to speak correctly in public, how to write acceptably, and how to conduct himself as a gentleman. To compensate for this lack of schooling, George trained himself. He studied books on math and on decorum, including *Rules of Civility & Decent Behaviour in Company and Conversation*, a sixteenth-century training manual written by French Jesuits for young noblemen. At age sixteen, Washington copied all 110 rules into his schoolbook. He followed these dictums so completely throughout his life that biographers consider them to be a major formative influence. The rules spanned every facet of everyday living, from table manners to profane language to advice on how to pick your friends. Here's a selection:

> *1st   Every Action done in Company, ought to be with Some Sign of Respect, to those that are Present.*

5th   If You Cough, Sneeze, Sigh, or Yawn, do it not Loud but Privately; and Speak not in your Yawning, but put Your handkercheif or Hand before your face and turn aside.

6th   Sleep not when others Speak, Sit not when others stand, Speak not when you Should hold your Peace, walk not on when others Stop.

17th   Be no Flatterer, neither Play with any that delights not to be Play'd Withal.

19th   let your Countenance be pleasant but in Serious Matters Somewhat grave.

22d   Shew not yourself glad at the Misfortune of another though he were your enemy.

23d   When you see a Crime punished, you may be inwardly Pleased; but always shew Pity to the Suffering Offender.

56th   Associate yourself with Men of good Quality if you Esteem your own Reputation; for 'tis better to be alone than in bad Company.

58th   Let your Conversation be without Malice or Envy, for 'tis a Sig[n o]f a Tractable and Commendable Nature: And in all Causes of Passion [ad]mit Reason to Govern.

109th   Let your Recreations be Manfull not Sinfull.

110th   Labour to keep alive in your Breast that Little Spark of Ce[les]tial fire Called Conscience.

If Washington learned poise and etiquette from *Rules of Civility*, he learned the virtues of controlling his anger from Seneca's *Morals*. Most of his early anger was directed toward his controlling mother, who was always telling him what he wasn't allowed to do. So the following words written by Seneca were relevant to young George (and would be relevant, presumably, to most teenagers from colonial to modern times): "A huge deal of time is spent in caviling about words and captions, disputations that work us up to an edge and then nothing comes of it." George copied these texts, too, in longhand into his boyhood schoolbooks, learning handwriting at the same time he learned proper conduct, ethics, and etiquette.

As a young man he was also influenced by the play *Cato*, written by Joseph Addison in 1713. *Cato* is based on the story of Cato the Younger (95–46 B.C.), a statesman and stoic in ancient Rome who opposed

✳

Print showing a young George Washington leading a group of boys with swords lifted in a mock charge as another group of boys advances in the background. Even as a youth, Washington was big for his age. He was an excellent horseman and wrestler, and he was proud of his throwing ability.

Caesar's imperial ambitions. He sided with Pompey in an unsuccessful civil war. In the play, Cato ends up committing suicide rather than submit to Caesar. Cato's words—"A day, an hour, of virtuous liberty is worth a whole eternity in bondage"—would prove prescient for Washington. The play's protaganist set a strong example for a man to whom the heavy weight of imperialism would become all too familiar. He included lines from the play in his farewell address and in letters he wrote throughout his life. The officers' wives put on *Cato* during the long, cold 1777 encampment at Valley Forge to inspire and entertain the troops. By then, Washington could have mouthed the words along with the performers.

Another part of George's self-imposed education consisted of emulating his half brother Lawrence, who came back from combat and married into the wealthy Fairfax family. He lived the life of a Virginia gentleman at Mount Vernon, the estate on the Potomac River that George would eventually inherit. The Fairfaxes took a liking to George when he visited his older half brother there during summers and holidays. The feeling was mutual. Oxford-educated Thomas Fairfax was the first English nobleman George had ever met.

The boy got his first view of British upper-class life— and he liked what he saw. He found he was naturally gifted at such gentlemanly pursuits as playing loo and whist in the parlor, dancing at balls, and riding to hounds. He learned how to dress in the latest fashion, and he developed a liking for the high-society lifestyle, as well as a crush on Sally Fairfax, a girl his age.

But George did not pursue this lifestyle to its hilt. According to historian W. W. Abbot,

> *He did not hang about in Williamsburg, riot at the College, play the young blade. Although he developed a passion for fox hunting and dancing, at both of which he became consummately skillful, and he always had to hold in check his love of gambling, the life he led as an adolescent and young adult meant the visiting back and forth, the balls, the horse races, and card playing had, in large part, to be deferred to a later day.*

At age twenty-one, when George heard that the king of England was looking for young men to help defend the colonies against the French and the Indians, he jumped at the chance to prove himself to the

British army. Though his schoolbooks showed an impressive knowledge of advanced mathematics, George was always happiest following physical pursuits. He once boasted that he had tossed a stone to the top of Natural Bridge, a stone arch in the Blue Ridge Mountains 215 feet above the ground.

It was around this time that George perfected his riding skills, which were highly thought of by others. Thomas Jefferson would later remark that Washington was the "best horseman of the age."

"As a teenage boy in the 1740s, he was a head taller than most boys his age. Were it not for his physical prowess in sports, one way boys settle such difference, his height could have marked him as somewhat of a freak," wrote Willard Sterne Randall in his book *George Washington: A Life*. Randall noted Washington's horsemanship abilities, as well as other physical traits. "He was an uncommonly good wrestler and rail-splitter, activities which, like riding, require great strength, control, and endurance. He was especially proud of his throwing arm."

By the time he was twenty-one, Washington had grown to his full height of six feet four inches, and had become a skilled surveyor. He knew how to navigate the Virginia woods, an expertise the British would need in order to fare well against the French in the French and Indian War, as the Seven Years War in North America was known. His mother tried to forbid him from becoming a soldier, but George went against her wishes and rode his horse to Williamsburg to present himself to the governor of the colonies. (*Rules of Civility* said nothing about obeying an overbearing mother.)

George went on to lead major victories in the French and Indian War, so he was disappointed when he didn't receive much recognition from the Brits. He was appointed commander in chief of the Virginia militia, but that actually gave him little power, since he was outranked by every officer in the British army. Red-coated officers took advantage of their position and commandeered the Virginian troops' supplies at the drop of a hat. When Washington requested that his Virginia regiment be enrolled in the regular British army to avoid these conflicts, the higher-ups refused. This enraged Washington. Though his standing was solid among Virginians, he was beginning to realize that the English would always see him as a lesser citizen, as a colonist. He felt that he and his regiment were being treated unfairly. He resigned his commission in the Virginia militia in 1759.

✳

William Howe, on the other hand, had no problem gaining a commission in the British imperial army. In 1746, when he was seventeen, his family bought him one. William catapulted through the ranks, becoming a lieutenant at eighteen, a captain at twenty-one, and a lieutenant colonel at twenty-eight. He distinguished himself for his courage and leadership along the coast of France during the Seven Years War, or the French and Indian War, where his battalion was once described as "the best trained . . . in all America." He was a strict disciplinarian but popular with his men, and was known for possessing bravery, energy, and integrity. He earned a reputation as a skilled tactician during an attack on Quebec.

At home, William became a national figure and a war hero—at six feet tall, he was strong, dark, and silent. He was known for his economy of words. That seemed to change after his oldest brother, George Augustus, lost his life leading a skirmish against

French forces at Fort Ticonderoga in 1758. William admired and respected his oldest brother and his death affected William greatly. He turned to gambling and drinking, and he began to spend more time around the faro tables in London, keeping company with that city's gamblers and courtesans. His older brother, Richard, spent his free time studying military tactics; William spent it gambling and in the company of loose women. His brothers and sisters called him "the savage," but it's not known whether this nickname referred to his primitive lifestyle or to the buckskins and Indian moccasins he brought home from America after the Seven Years War. There's no record what his attractive wife, the sister of a wealthy Anglo-Irish politician, thought about all this. Friends of the Howes wrote of Mrs. Howe's love for her husband and her loneliness when he went away on military missions, but if there were letters from her to her husband, they all went up in flames with the rest of his papers.

By day Willaim had a new role, representing the town of Nottingham in Parliament where, in the 1770s, there was much debate about how to handle the empire's colonies. Like the rest of his fellow Whigs, William grew more and more strongly opposed to his king's opinion that the rights of Englishmen must not extend to colonial Americans. In 1774, Howe told the electors of Nottingham that the monarchy had pushed its American policy too far, that the British army would not conquer America, and that he would refuse a command there if offered one. But when King George III asked him to go and join the effort, duty and his allegiance to the king won out. William reluctantly agreed to serve, on the condition that he would resolve the dispute by peaceful means if possible, and by war if necessary.

William wrote, "My going thither was not of my seeking. I was ordered and could not refuse. . . . Every man's private feelings ought to give way to the service of the public." Howe was bowing to imperialism just as Washington was bristling in the face of its inequities. And just as it was impossible for Howe to refuse to serve a monarch whose fruits he and his family had been reaping all of their lives, it was impossible for Washington to refuse the position of commander in chief of America's Continental army. In *Common*

Sense, Thomas Paine wrote, "To know whether it be the interest of this continent to be Independent, we need only to ask this simple question: Is it the interest of a man to be a boy all his life?" Washington thought not.

※

Dogs in Early America

There's a famous quote from Dostoyevsky: "The degree of civilization in a society can be measured by entering its prisons." It's likely that a more canine-minded observer might have sought out the same findings by looking at the laws a society passes to protect its dogs. And in late-eighteenth-century England and its colonies, there were some strict dog-protecting laws. According to encyclopedist Abraham Rees, in a compendium published in Philadelphia in 1805, a mastiff was considered valuable enough that the calf-sized beast was lawfully spared even if it was tearing another dog to death. George III pronounced that the stealing of dogs merited a fine of twenty to thirty pounds (a lot of money back then) or an imprisonment of six to twelve months. For subsequent offenses, the fine grew to thirty to fifty pounds, or on nonpayment, imprisonment of up to eighteen months, plus a public whipping.

The British, as well as the English settlers in America, bemoaned the way dogs were treated in other, less civilized lands. "The dog is our servant but he is also our companion and friend," Rees wrote,

> *but the good qualities of this animal, though uniformly felt, are not invariably acknowledged. In England, the dog is cherished and protected, but there are many parts of the world, not even to instance the more uncivilized states, where the condition of these ill-fated animals may justly excite our commiseration; countries in which the most solid and beneficial advantages are derived to society from their zeal and industry, and in reward for which they receive only the most inhuman and ungrateful treatment, detestation and contempt.*

The animal-rights movement got its start in Britain as early as the 1780s. It was pioneered by a man named Richard Martin, or "Humanity Dick," who, like Washington, kept various types of dogs for hunting on his huge estate. He also allowed some of the pups inside his house and treated them as pets. Some speculate that his close relationship with his dogs was in direct proportion to his less-than-close relationship with his wife, Elizabeth. Richard traveled a lot to fulfill his duties as a member of Parliament from the county of Galway, and while he was gone, his wife tended to gravitate toward other, more geographically accessible partners. It was rumored that Richard was not the father of at least one of their children. He ended up divorcing Elizabeth after one of her affairs became public. All of this marital discord just pushed him closer to his pups. The turning point may have been an episode in 1783, when a local landlord nicknamed "Fighting" Fitzgerald shot a friend's dog. Martin attempted to avenge that dog by challenging Fitzgerald to a duel. He went on to propose a bill in the House of Commons that was designed to make animal cruelty punishable by law.

Englishmen found it especially detestable that in

many countries, dog flesh was considered food. So did the colonists, presumably, although they had no problem employing short-haired terriers as "turnspit dogs," to replace the "spit-turning boys" whose job it was to rotate the spit on which a cut of meat was roasting over an open fire. The turnspit dogs were good-natured short-legged terriers bred expressly for the purpose of running on a treadmill that was belted to a spit.

Forcing a terrier to work a treadmill may reek of cruelty to modern citizens, but assigning each breed of dog a functional purpose was regular practice in the late eighteenth century. Only a few select breeds were meant to exist exclusively as pets. These breeds' inherent lack of utility made them symbols of luxury and affluence. They acted as accessories for those wealthy enough to lead a life of leisure. The smaller the lapdog, the more pleasing it was for the lady who carried him in her arms, and piled him with his fellow pups on her bed, on her divan, and in her carriage. These dogs did serve a few practical purposes, namely to act as living heating pads to ease cramps and stomachaches, and to attract fleas so they wouldn't land on nearby humans.

The ladies at Padua favored pugs. Other lapdogs were the Maltese and the Comforter, each of whom acted as "a general attendant on the ladies at the toilette or in the drawing room." (There was a legend circulated around this time that a dog belonging to a nobleman in the Medici family always attended his master's table, changed his plates for him, and carried his wine to him in a glass on a silver tray—without spilling a drop. One dog near Saxony was said to know and be able to speak thirty words.) Too bad Comforters couldn't fetch wine—that might have prompted encyclopedist Abraham Rees to overlook their tendency to be "of a snappish, ill-natured disposition, and very noisy." Dalmatians were considered good carriage companions (maybe because they were lousy hunters). King Charles spaniels, by decree of King Charles in the mid seventeenth century, were allowed in any public place, even in the Houses of Parliament, where animals were not usually permitted. But besides these few breeds, dogs were as utilitarian as horses, cows, sheep, and chickens.

The Siberian or Greenland dog drew sledges over frozen snow. The Newfoundland dog carried sleds stacked high with wood. Water dogs with webbed feet hunted ducks and were sent overboard after any little thing that happened to fall into the water. Irish greyhounds could hunt and kill wolves. (Canute, king of the English, Danes, and Norwegians in the 1000s, declared that no one under the rank of a gentleman should presume to keep a greyhound.) Foxhounds and terriers were a vital part of foxhunting. The hounds chased and caught the fox unless it escaped down a hole. If that happened, a terrier was sent down to scare the fox out of the hole or to kill the prey underground.

George Washington's love for foxhunting is so well known that he is sometimes credited as being the father of American foxhunting. In fact, this isn't true—the first pack of foxhunting hounds was brought to Maryland by Reverend Robert Brooke in 1650. But Washington's fondness for the hunt did do much to publicize the sport, and its popularity grew throughout the eighteenth century, mostly in the Southern and Middle Atlantic states. Washington loved to "ride to his hounds," or foxhunt in the mornings on a formal hunt or casually on his own when he set out to inspect his eight thousand acres of farms.

"In 1768, Washington went to church on fifteen days, mostly when away from home, and hunted foxes on forty-nine," wrote James Thomas Flexner in his Pulitzer Prize–winning biography *Washington: The Indispensable Man.* "Sometimes he took his hounds along when he rode around his farms, gleefully abandoning business if they started a fox."

When Washington or another gentleman farmer threw an organized hunting party, it usually started at breakfast and ended with a champagne lunch. The wives and other enthusiastic ladies would sometimes participate, but mostly they watched and cheered. Just like modern cocktail parties and power lunches, these events were opportunities for people to form and solidify political and social alliances. They served as venues for deal-making and political campaigning, and as a place for men and women to meet and flirt and make romantic connections. In most cases, slaves handled the dogs. Slaves redirected the animals (which might include any combination of fox, rabbit, squirrel, quail, duck, pheasant, raccoon, bear, turkey, or deer) during the hunt, pointing them toward the kill, and they also dressed the prey.

Through hunting, hounds developed the reputation for being intelligent, sagacious, tenacious, and affectionate. Unfortunately, keeping dogs in heat away from improper sires was more of a problem in the American colonies than it was in England and Europe, since there were lots of curs and mutts around. Before the Revolution, Washington began the practice of searching out the best dogs possible, even if it meant breeding them himself.

"The breeding of horses and hounds was a perpetual concern," Flexner writes. "Several times [Washington] noted ruefully in one of his diaries that he had been outwitted by some household pet. . . ."

✳

According to the United Kennel Club, Thomas Walker of Albemarle County, Virginia, imported hounds from England in 1742. George Washington also imported several hounds from England in 1770. These dogs became the foundation strains of the "Virginia hounds," which were developed into the Walker hound, as the strain is known today.

Washington's efforts, especially before the war, were well rewarded. While eschewing politics publicly, he was shrewder than most behind the scenes. Exchanges and loans of hounds served to solidify political and social relationships.

However, Washington didn't seem to let his hound-exchanges muddy his political views. He borrowed from and lent to his Virginian neighbor Bryan Fairfax before and after the war of independence, even though Fairfax was a Loyalist. This letter from Fairfax to Washington, dated July 15, 1772, shows that their opinions of hounds differed as much as their views of the monarchy:

If it should happen that either of the Hounds sent down lately should not please you I beg to have the first offer of them; I mention this because I am convinced that all Sportsmen do not look on Dogs in the same Light, of which you are also satisfied from the many superexcellent dogs you have had given you, which have not answered yr. Expectation. Some allowance must be made for prejudice, perhaps therefore you'll not think Rouser equal to Ringwood, tho' I do expect that he is closemouthed. Dabster tho' a great Babbler at first I liked the best of the three; which I mention lest he should at first for want of Practice return to his Babbling and you should condemn him too soon. Tho' you did not seem to like Ranger I really think he was as good a Dog as ever I had except his want of a good Nose—Rouser is exactly such another in every Respect. Two of my hounds running a Fox yesterday a great part of the day hath revived the Subject in my Mind & hath caused this postscript.

※

Dogs at War

Dogs were found to be as useful for sniffing out humans as they were for sniffing out foxes. In 1755, Benjamin Franklin was concerned about the attacks by Shawnee and Delaware Indians on the settlements close to Boston. Towns and villages were being raided and burned, their inhabitants murdered. In a letter to a friend, Franklin suggested a strategy for using dogs to hunt down the attackers:

> *Dogs should be used against the Indians. They should be large, strong and fierce; and every dog*

led in a slip string, to prevent their tiring themselves by running out and in, and discovering the party by barking at squirrels, etc. Only when the party come near thick woods and suspicious places they should turn out a dog or two to search them. In case of meeting a party of the enemy, the dogs are all then to be turned loose and set on. They will be fresher and finer for having been previously confined and will confound the enemy a good deal and be very serviceable. This was the Spanish method of guarding their marches.

He pointed out that dogs had been used effectively during the Spanish Conquest.

But no action was taken, not even in 1764, when John Penn, the lieutenant governor of Pennsylvania, proposed in a letter to James Young, paymaster and commissioner of muster, that "every Soldier be allowed three shillings per month, who brings with him a strong dog, that shall be judged proper to be employed in discovering and pursuing the savages." In 1779, another plea for war dogs was made by William McClay of Pennsylvania's Supreme Executive Council. "I have sustained some ridicule for a scheme, which I have long recommended, that of hunting the scalping parties with horsemen and dogs," he wrote, recalling that "it was in this manner, that the Indians were extirpated out of whole [countries] in South America." Perhaps someone in power decided that tracking humans like animals was inhumane. That's certainly what a number of Quakers thought more than a half-century later, when word got out about General Zachary Taylor loosing a pack of thirty-three Cuban-bred bloodhounds to sniff out Seminole Indians and runaway slaves in the Florida War of 1835. The Quakers filed petitions with Congress, strongly protesting the use of these bloodhounds.

The war of 1835 marked the first time the U.S. army recorded the use of dogs in any official manner. But it wouldn't have been an anomaly of military history had America used dogs to supplement manpower earlier. Ancient Persians, Greeks, and Babylonians used attack dogs at war. Ancient Roman writers such as Plutarch and Pliny the Elder wrote of fierce dogs who would fearlessly face off against men and their swords. In the fifth century, Attila the Hun apparently made so much use of battle dogs that they had their own doggy armor—battle plates and chains. In 1695, the British unleashed one hundred savage dogs on uprising slaves in Jamaica.

Napoléon Bonaparte had a love-hate relationship with dogs. The eighteenth-century emperor developed an aversion to his wife Josephine's canines when the wealthy widow refused to kick her fawn-colored pug, Fortune, out of bed on their wedding night. Josephine was even more attached to Fortune than to her other pugs and spaniels because the pooch had helped her escape the guillotine. The pup had visited her in prison every day during the French Revolution, and Josephine hid messages addressed to highly placed individuals under his velvet collar. The messages asked for the recipients to arrange for the delay of her execution. Who could blame a woman for giving this lifesaving dog special treatment? But Napoléon didn't understand the point of letting a pug into their private chambers, especially after the dog bit his calf while he and his bride were consummating their marriage. He bore the scars from that wound for the rest of his life.

Josephine wanted her dogs around constantly, even while she was traveling. A select pug would even get his own carriage, his own personal maid, and a cashmere shawl and valuable carpet to rest upon during a trip. Later, when the jealous Napoléon suspected that his wife was having an affair with a man named Hippolyte Charles, he erupted with anger when he saw Fortune's affection for Charles. Napoléon took this as evidence that the man had been in Josephine's (and Fortune's) bed. When he became emperor, he passed legislation forbidding anyone to name a dog Napoléon.

Napoléon never took Josephine's dogs to battle—but he was known to use other dogs as weapons, or at least as sentinels. On a campaign in Egypt in 1798, he ordered all the local dogs rounded up and chained along the walls of Alexandria to warn his troops of an attack. And a year later, he wrote to one of his generals, advising that he, too, post a bevy of canines in front of his fort in order to warn of the enemy's arrival and delay their attack. Late in his life, when he was in exile and spending his time recording accounts of his days in battle, he wrote of one instance when he was especially impressed by the strong bond between man and dog. It happened at the end of a battle, while he was looking over a field littered with corpses. Next to one slain soldier sat a dog, licking his master's wounds and leaping back and forth between Napoléon and the corpse as if to say, "Look at my master. Look what he's sacrificed for your reputation." Or maybe the dog was hopeful that the emperor could bring his master back to life. Whatever the case, Napoléon was profoundly moved. He wrote:

> *Perhaps it was the spirit of the time and the place that affected me. But I assure you no occurrence of any of my other battlefields impressed me so keenly. I halted on my tour to gaze on the spectacle, and reflect on its meaning.*
>
> *This soldier, I realized, must have had friends at home and in his regiment; yet he lay there deserted by all except his dog. . . . I had looked on, unmoved, at battles which decided the future of nations. Tearless, I had given orders which brought death to thousands.*
>
> *Yet, here I was, stirred, profoundly stirred, stirred to tears. And by what? By the grief of one dog. I am certain that at that instant I felt more ready than at any other time to show mercy toward a suppliant foeman. I could understand just then the tinge of mercy which*

*led Achilles to yield the corpse of his enemy,
Hector, to the weeping Priam.*

The practice of soldiers looking to dogs for camaraderie and support is centuries old. Dogs saved the life of Robert, William the Conqueror's son, and the lives of his soldiers during the First Crusade (1095–1099). When their horses and mules died from starvation, harsh conditions, and enemy raids, Robert used his dogs to transport weapons and supplies.

During the American Civil War (1861–1865), dogs accompanied both Union and Confederate soldiers as makeshift messengers, sentries, guards, and maybe most important, companions. When a man left home to report for military duty, chances were he wouldn't be back for months, maybe even years. His only communication with family and loved ones was through letter writing, and the postal system was highly unreliable. It made sense to bring a pet as a reminder of home and as a living, breathing substitute for his faraway family. These dogs often became mascots to entire regiments.

One famous Civil War mascot was Sallie, a brindle

Staffordshire bull terrier, who joined the 11th Pennsylvania Volunteer Infantry regiment as a four-week-old puppy in the early days of the war. She grew up among the men of the regiment, hanging out with them while they camped between battles, following them on marches and even onto the battlefield. She was fiercely loyal to her unit. During skirmishes, she'd hold her position on the line and bark at the enemy. During the first day of the Battle of Gettysburg, Sallie was separated from her unit. Unable to find them, she returned to their former position at the Union battle line at Oak Ridge, where she stood guard over the casualties, licking the wounds of the injured and watching over the dead. Days later, after the Confederates retreated from the field, she was found weakened and malnourished, amid the dead and debris. A compassionate soldier recognized her and returned Sallie to her unit.

She avoided injury until May 8, 1864, when she was shot in the neck in the line of duty. A surgeon at the field hospital pronounced that she would live but that the bullet could not be removed. Sallie returned to active duty a few days later, sporting an impressive battle scar, and she continued to serve until February 6,

1865, when she was shot in the head at the battle of Hatcher's Run, Virginia. The Union men buried her on the field of battle under heavy enemy fire. Sallie is memorialized at the 11th Pennsylvania monument in Gettysburg, Pennsylvania. Other war mascots disappeared from their units when they were taken as prisoners of war. Jack, the brown-and-white bull terrier mascot of the 102nd Pennsylvania Infantry, was captured twice. The second time, he was exchanged for a Confederate soldier.

During the Civil War, dogs were also used on both sides as sentries, to sniff out prison-camp escapees. Enormous hounds stood guard at Andersonville Prison in Atlanta, Georgia, and at Libby Prison and Castle Thunder Prison in Richmond, Virginia. These hounds were truly savage, and being caught by one of them meant death. The biggest was Hero, who weighed in at 198 pounds and measured seven feet long and thirty-eight inches high.

Much less is recorded about the dogs of the American Revolution than about the canine mascots and sentries of the Civil War. Despite the suggestions made by Franklin, Penn, and McClay to adopt dogs as soldiers, canines were never charged with hunting and tracking the enemy. But soldiers and officers did maintain dogs as pets during the 1775–1783 ordeal, just as soldiers did years later in the mid-1800s. As in the Civil War, they were probably valued as reminders of home and as sources of companionship.

※

In art-history circles, the depiction of a dog can have various meanings. In eighteenth-century portraiture, dogs symbolize loyalty, especially when the painting is of a husband and wife (loyalty to each other) or of a widow (loyalty to the memory of her dead husband). Kings, princes, and soldiers are pictured with large, powerful dogs as signs of their own power and strength. This was probably not the case with the portraits of Napoléon and his dachshunds. In these paintings, the dogs' rendering in oil was more a matter of immortalizing their master's adoration, and perhaps unintentionally, his tender side.

What about the presence of a dog in a military man's life? Does this signify humanity and compassion? Another historical figure, the German armored-division commander Erwin Rommel, of the Second World War, also kept dachshunds. Was it possible that Rommel possessed an ounce of compassion? The only answer is no answer—that there is no singular meaning: Dogs may or may not announce a person's capacity for loyalty, strength, or humanity. But it is a truism that dogs can change the course of history. Perhaps Napoléon's encounter with that slain soldier and his loyal dog led him to act compassionately in some later scenario. In his book *The Pawprints of History*, Stanley Coren proposes that George Washington attained his post as commander in chief of the Continental army as the result of a series of events that began with—what else?—a dog.

FOUR

✳

Sweet Lips Gets Washington a Job

George Washington was having a hard time adjusting to Philadelphia when he arrived to serve as a Virginia delegate in the Second Continental Congress in the fall of 1775. Since retiring from the military life in 1759, Washington had married a wealthy widow named Martha Custis and settled down at Mount Vernon, where he'd spent so much time as a boy with his half brother Lawrence and the Fairfaxes. The affinity for foxhunting he'd shown back then had developed into a full-blown hobby, complete with extensive animal accoutrements.

--- ✳ ---

Martha Dandridge Custis Washington was born at Chestnut Grove in New Kent County, Virginia, on June 2, 1731. Her father, John Dandridge, had originally immigrated to Virginia from England. Martha married Colonel Daniel Parke Custis in 1750, and they had four children: Daniel, in 1751; Frances, in 1753; John (Jacky), in 1755; and Martha (Patsy), in 1756 or 1757. Unfortunately, Daniel lived only three years, Frances four. Then on July 26, 1757, when Martha was just twenty-six years old, her husband died suddenly. A year and a half later, on January 6, 1759, she married Colonel George Washington. George and Martha and her surviving children, Jacky and Patsy, moved to Mount Vernon in April of that year, and it would remain George and Martha's home until their deaths. Although Martha liked dogs as much as George, she and he did not always share the same affections for the same dogs.

"Perhaps the most jarring picture [of Washington]," wrote acclaimed historian Joseph Ellis in his biography *His Excellency*, was the fact that in truth, diametrically opposed to his persona of "public virtue," Washington was an "indulged Virginia gentleman for whom the phrase 'pursuit of happiness' meant galloping to hounds.

"And the foxhunt was not just a metaphor. According to his diary, Washington spent two and five hours a day for forty-nine days in 1768 on horseback pursuing the elusive fox," Ellis continued. "He also devoted considerable energy to breeding his hounds, who frequently confounded him with their ingenuity at linking up—what he called 'lining'—with partners of their own choosing."

At Mount Vernon, Washington had lavish stables of horses and kennels full of hounds. He was very involved with his hounds, breeding them and even giving them names such as Sweet Lips, Venus, Music, Lady, Truelove, Taster, Tipsy, Tippler, and Drunkard. But at his temporary residence in Philadelphia, there was no room for his horses and hounds and little opportunity to go foxhunting. Having his hound Sweet Lips along as a companion was some compensation.

Walking Sweet Lips one day through the city streets, he ran into Elizabeth Powel, the wife of the mayor of Philadelphia, who stopped to admire both Washington and his handsome dog. (It seems that dogs have always been magnets for attracting the fairer sex.) Powel went home and told her husband about the man whose acquaintance she had made on the street, and Samuel Powel decided that the Virginian delegate would be a worthy addition to his growing political network. The couple invited Washington for dinner, and they discussed the Virginian's disappointment with not being able to ride to the hounds as often as he was used to. The Powels made it possible for Washington to visit the Gloucester Hunting Club in New Jersey, directly across the river from Philadelphia.

Washington made fast friends with Powel and the other men at the hunting club. They bonded over their shared love of the hunt, and Washington gifted some of these gentlemen with black-and-tan hunting hounds of the breed he himself had discovered by mixing Irish, German, and English hounds. These were powerful men who had the ears of other powerful men, and it was they who lobbied for Washington to be offered the command of the Continental army in June 1775. So perhaps it was thanks to a dog named Sweet Lips that Washington happened to lead the Americans to victory in the Revolution and, later, serve as the fledgling nation's first president.

※

Washington didn't get off to a great start as commander in chief of the Continental army. He took command on July 3, 1775, after the Americans' loss at the Battle of Bunker Hill, and from then until his heroic crossing of the Delaware River on Christmas Day 1777, he lost battle after battle to General William Howe and his redcoats. It was miraculous that Washington maintained enough manpower, and his men enough morale, to continue with the war even after all of these defeats. This is one of the mysteries of the American Revolution. There's a saying that is sometimes credited to Lafayette: "Any other general than Howe would have beaten Washington, and any other general than Washington would have beaten Howe." Howe seemed reluctant to impose the full force of the British army on the rebels—after winning a battle, he seemed always to hang back and let Wash-

This painting by John Ward Dunsmore depicts Washington returning from a hunt on the grounds of his beloved Mount Vernon.

ington and his troops retreat to safety. Washington continued to escape from close calls.

One of these close calls was at the Battle of Long Island in August 1776. General Howe's brother, Lord Admiral Richard Howe, had arrived a month earlier with reinforcements—thirty thousand British redcoats and Hessian mercenaries from Germany. As soon as Lord Howe arrived, he and his brother set out to negotiate for peace with the colonists. As Whigs, they were more interested in settling the conflict with a compromise than in crushing the ragtag American militia underfoot with their superior supplies and greater numbers of men. Lord Howe was so confident in his mission that he predicted peace would be declared in no fewer than ten days after his arrival. But he and his brother underestimated the colonists' stubbornness. They also realized that they were unequipped to negotiate for peace. The only power given them by the king was to grant pardons to those who decided to return to allegiance and to grant amnesty to communities that laid down their arms.

The Howe brothers sent a note to Washington, enclosing a copy of a declaration of the royal clemency and the message that the king would grant a free pardon to all penitents. But the letter was addressed to "George Washington, Esq."—it didn't bear his official title of commander in chief. Washington saw this as a snub to both himself and to the legitimacy of the colonists' military outfit. He refused to receive the letter. A second letter was sent, and again it was refused—but, always the Southern gentleman, Washington invited the major who delivered it into the American camp for lunch. Having gotten wind of the letter's contents, Washington said, "Having committed no fault, we need no pardon. We are only defending what we deem to be our indisputable rights." He wasn't interested in clemency or pardons, and since this was all the Howes were empowered to offer, they realized that they might actually have to fight this war.

The addition of the reinforcements who sailed over with Lord Howe made the British army more than thirty thousand strong. Washington's consisted of about eleven thousand men in the summer of 1776, and it mushroomed to seventeen thousand after he appealed to the colonies. That August, on Long Island, the Brits fell on the American troops and laid waste to their ranks. After the battle, Washington anxiously watched the British to see if they would follow up their victory by capturing the rest of the much weakened American army—which could well have meant the end of the war. But Howe seemed to be too busy celebrating his victory to bother, and the Americans beat a quick retreat in boats concealed by a heavy fog. About this debacle, American general Israel Putnam wrote that Howe was either "a friend of America or no general."

Less than a month later, on September 16, Howe won a skirmish against Washington's troops at Harlem Heights, in a field that lies near where Columbia University stands today. The battle ended at about three in the afternoon, after Howe added so many reinforcements that the Americans started to retreat. Historians point out that Howe could have encircled the American army from the north and cut off their only means of escape from the island of Manhattan to the mainland. Instead, Howe concentrated on occupying New York and, essentially, let the Americans off the hook once more.

After winning this series of battles and controlling the city of New York by the end of September, Howe would have been happy to call it a campaign and declare a hiatus for the winter months. Unfortunately for him, the Continental army was wreaking havoc on Loyalists in New Jersey, and it was the redcoats' job to protect these loyal subjects of the king. A column of 4,500 redcoats, led by Lord Cornwallis, surprised the Americans at Fort Lee, and they retreated in so much haste that they abandoned camp without dousing their kettle fires. Cornwallis continued to pursue them, intending to run them into the ground, when a messenger of Howe's came along and informed him that any further movement was to wait until Howe arrived with reinforcements. A day went by, then two days, then three. Howe didn't arrive until a week later, and all he brought with him was a single brigade.

The American army was ragtag, limping, and fast losing morale. The year 1776 was the worst for the Continental army. It was reported that Washington lost about ten thousand men from sickness. One thousand more soldiers were killed in battle, twelve thousand were wounded, and six thousand were taken prisoner. Once a man was wounded, there was little chance for survival. The army camps were filthy. The Americans had typhus and smallpox, with little or no medical services available. The field hospitals were hothouses for widespread infection. The sick and wounded were laid on lice-infested straw—head to toe and row after row. And neither British nor American surgeons had knowledge of anesthetics. The wounded were given a lead bullet to bite down on during operations. Surgeons used unsterilized knives and meat saws to amputate limbs—and hot tar to cauterize the stumps.

As the weather was getting colder, the Americans' uniforms were getting more threadbare. The leather on their shoes was wearing thin. So it's not surprising that it took Washington's army a week to retreat from Cornwallis's troops. The last of them were pushing off from the banks of the Delaware when the redcoats rode up. An officer in Howe's army wrote, "General Howe appeared to have calculated with the greatest accuracy the exact time necessary for the enemy to make his escape."

FIVE

The Gentleman's Code

I f Washington ever recorded his opinion of Howe, that letter or diary entry didn't survive. Alexander Hamilton, Washington's aide-de-camp, wrote in a letter to Gouverneur Morris in 1777 that Howe was an "unintelligible gentleman" and that no rule of interpretation could "possibly be found out by which to unravel his designs." Maybe Washington felt the same. He could have agreed with John Adams, who wrote to his wife that it was "impossible to discover the designs of an enemy who has no design at all."

The letters that passed between Howe and Washington were polite, detached, and formal. Sometimes there was an undercurrent of exasperation, as when Washington was lamenting a lack of reply concerning a pressing matter or when they wrangled over the exchange of prisoners. Mostly, though, each respected the other's standing as general, and it's possible that if they hadn't been enemies they might have been friends. Both were fond of cards and gambling. Washington's diaries speak frequently of his winnings and losses at cards and even mention little wagers that he placed on horse races and cockfights. Both liked to drink—at a dinner held for members of the first Continental Congress by the city of Philadelphia, Washington was, famously, still on his feet after thirty-six toasts. And both seemed to agree that civility and the gentleman's code were important to uphold even during a time of war.

There are several possible explanations for Howe's unwillingness to close the deal after the battles of Long Island, Harlem Heights, and New Jersey in the late fall of 1777. Some of his peers regarded him as indolent, more interested in socializing in the game halls and ballrooms of New York City than in winning the war. It was well known that he kept a mistress while he was in America, a "flashing blonde" named Elizabeth Lloyd

Loring, the young wife of New Englander Joshua Loring. Howe appointed Joshua Loring his commissioner of prisoners, which was convenient, since the commissioner of prisoners often traveled with the general. In this case, so did his wife. One satirist of the period obviously thought that Howe's impotence in battle was directly linked to his overzealousness in other spheres:

Awake, arouse, Sir Billy,
There's forage in the plain,
Ah, leave your little Filly,
And open the campaign.
Heed not a woman's prattle
Which tickles in the ear,
But give the word for battle,
And grasp the warlike spear.

Howe and Mrs. Loring also made it into the ditty "The Battle of the Kegs," written by Frances Hopkinson. In the fall of 1777, a group of patriots floated kegs filled with gunpowder down the Delaware River toward Philadelphia, where British ships were anchored. One of the kegs struck a British barge, killing four men. The redcoats on deck couldn't tell where the explosions were coming from, so they started to shoot in all directions. Here are some of the verses from Hopkinson's song:

> *Gallants, attend, and hear a friend*
> *Trill forth harmonious ditty.*
> *Strange things I'll tell, which late befell*
> *In Philadelphia city.*
> *'Twas early day, as poets say,*
> *Just when the sun was rising.*
> *A soldier stood on a log of wood*
> *And saw a sight surprising.*
>
> *As in amaze he stood to gaze;*
> *The truth can't be denied, sirs.*
> *He spied a score of kegs or more*
> *Come floating down the tide, sirs.*
> *A sailor, too, in jerkin blue,*
> *This strange appearance viewing,*
> *First damned his eyes in great surprise,*
> *Then said, "Some mischief's brewing.*
>
> *"These kegs, I'm told, the rebels hold,*
> *Packed up like pickled herring,*

And they're come down t'attack the town
In this new way of ferrying."
The soldier flew, the sailor, too,
And scared almost to death, sirs,
Wore out their shoes to spread the news,
And ran till out of breath, sirs.

Now up and down, throughout the town,
Most frantic scenes were acted;
And some ran here and some ran there,
Like men almost distracted.
Some "Fire" cried, which some denied,
But said the earth had quaked;
And girls and boys, with hideous noise,
Ran through the town half-naked.

Sir William, he, snug as a flea,
Lay all this time a-snoring;
Nor dreamed of harm, as he lay warm,
In bed with Mrs. Loring.
Now in a fright, he starts upright,
Awaked by such a clatter;
He rubs his eyes and boldly cries,
"For God's sake, what's the matter?"

It is important to note that it was apparent to all that Howe did not lack the necessary bravery of a field general. In fact, quite the opposite was true. He had distinguished himself before the war, but his performance at Bunker Hill sealed his reputation with his troops and his fellow commanders. In that battle, Howe led his troops up the hill against a fortified position. His regiment was pushed back several times by withering fire, but his troops reformed and charged each time, until the Americans were finally dislodged.

Christopher Ward reported in *The War of the Revolution*: "As they formed in lines to begin their ascent up the hill, Howe addressed the troops saying that he was honored to command them and he did not want one of them, 'to go a step further than where I go myself at your head.' He kept his promise to them, for in the grand tradition, he fought conspicuously in the front ranks the entire battle."

On June 25, 1777, General John Burgoyne wrote to Lord Stanley,

> *Howe's disposition was exceeding soldier-like; in my opinion it was perfect. As his first arm advanced up the hill, they met with a thousand*

impediments from strong fences, and were much exposed. They were also exceedingly hurt by musquetry from Charles-Town, though Clinton and I did not perceive it, till Howe sent us word by a boat, and desired us to set fire to the town, which was immediately done. We threw a parcel of shells, and the whole was instantly in flames. Our battery afterwards kept an incessant fire on the heights: it was seconded by a number of frigates, floating batteries, and one ship of the line.

And now ensued one of the greatest scenes of war that can be conceived: if we look to the height, Howe's corps ascending the hill in the face of entrenchments, and in a very disadvantageous ground, was much engaged; and to the left the enemy pouring in fresh troops by thousands . . .

Something to keep in mind was a quote from Howe, not long after the Battle of Bunker Hill. He wrote to Lord Germain, the British secretary of American affairs, ". . . the most essential duty I had to observe was not wantonly to commit His Majesty's troops, where the object was inadequate. I well knew that any considerable loss sustained by the army could not speedily, nor easily, be repaired." Indeed, Howe begged the British secretary for more troops throughout his prosecution of the war. He was repeatedly rebuffed, and slowly became angry with the secretary's planning of the war.

Washington himself was thoughtful of Howe's reluctance, and offered these thoughts in a letter to Joseph Reed on February 10, 1776, "I have been convinced, by General Howe's conduct, that he has either been very ignorant of our situation (which I do not believe) or that he has received positive orders (which, I think, is natural to conclude) not to put anything to hazard till his reinforcements arrive. . . ."

But from what we do know about Howe, it's very possible that his so-called indolence stemmed from the lack of enthusiasm he felt about the war. Before he even set sail in the *Cerberus* in the spring of 1775, he was less than gung-ho about the king's strategy. As a Whig, he empathized with the Americans and hoped for reconciliation. He had no desire to crush the patriots simply because they had the self-respect to fight for their rights.

Some of the British officers had an opposite out-look. They favored a strategy of flexing their military muscle to pound the colonials into the ground. They wanted to use extreme violence and terror in order to break the Americans' will to resist. Major John Pitcairn, Admiral Samuel Graves, and General John Burgoyne all recommended to Howe that they continue to burn New England towns until the colonists surrendered. Burgoyne directed his men to burn Charlestown. Graves did the same in Falmouth. But Howe forbade his men from acting this way, as did his brother, the admiral. In fact, General Howe ordered the execution of soldiers who attacked civilians or burned private property. Howe's second-in-command, General Henry Clinton, always wanted to destroy the rebel army completely, but for Howe, the war was a gentleman's game of maneuvering and taking advantage of situations as they became available. Imagine Clinton's frustration at the number of times Howe completely rejected his advice.

Howe played fair. A letter from Howe to General Washington on September 22, 1776, laments the fact that one of his men found "a ball cut and fixed to the end of a nail" at an American encampment. "I do not

make any comment upon such unwarrantable prac-
tices," he wrote, "being well assured the contrivance
has not come to your knowledge." Washington replied
that he, too, abhorred the contrivance and that this
was the first he'd seen or heard of it. "Every measure
shall be taken to prevent so wicked and infamous a
practice being adopted by this army," wrote Washington. These letters were exchanged one day after New
York had gone up in flames, presumably at the hands
of the British, but Washington said nothing about the
fire in his letters from that day. Maybe he suspected
that the fire was set on direct order not from Howe but
from another British officer.

Washington exhibited gentlemanly behavior, and
he expected the same from his army. He ordered his
troops to treat all animals well. He also issued a pro-
fanity order in August 1776 from his New York headquarters. It read, in part,

> *The General is sorry to be informed that the*
> *foolish, and wicked practice, of profane cursing*
> *and swearing (a Vice heretofore little known in*
> *an American Army) is growing into fashion; he*
> *hopes the officers will, by example, as well as*

influence, endeavour to check it, and that both they, and the men will reflect, that we can have little hopes of the blessing of Heaven on our Arms, if we insult it by our impiety, and folly; added to this, it is a vice so mean and low, without any temptation, that every man of sense, and character, detests and despises it.

Washington stayed true to *Rules of Civility* even during the war. (Rule number 49 reads, "Use no Reproachfull Language against any one neither Curse nor Revile.")

Gentlemanly behavior did not prevent the generals from trying to out-strategize each other. And at the end of 1776, Washington knew he had to do something drastic. After a series of defeats, columns of his men were going over to the enemy. The Revolution was unraveling. The general wrote to his brother, "I think the game is up." In December of that year, Howe and his army were ensconced in winter quarters—Howe was whooping it up in New York, and his troops were encamped all around. Washington knew that their guard would be down on Christmas Eve, so he led his army of 2,400 colonials through the ice floes that choked the Delaware River. The Americans were in bad shape. One young officer, Major James Wilkinson, wrote in his journal of the footprints leading down to the river, "tinged here and there with blood from the feet of the men who wore broken shoes." They pushed their sixty-foot-long barges off from shore at two in the afternoon and crossed silently from Pennsylvania to New Jersey. By eleven at night, a nasty nor'easter was spitting sleet and snow. By four in the morning, they had poled all the barges across the river, and Washington was organizing them into ranks to march ten miles down River Road to Trenton to surprise the 1,500 Hessian soldiers drunk and asleep in their barracks.

The colonials stormed the town, killing hundreds of stunned Hessians and suffering only four casualties themselves. After the British surrendered, the Americans captured the Hessian colonel Johann Rall. Washington was said to have been extremely courteous and considerate in his treatment of this man who had laid waste to his troops only a few weeks earlier. (Rule of Civility number 22: "Shew not yourself glad at the Misfortune of another though he were your enemy.") The Americans retreated to rest before the next battle as the British generals rounded up their forces to take on the triumphant rebels. Cornwallis was confident that he was bound "to bag the fox the next morning." But the Americans' morale was high from their victory at Trenton. News of it had spread, convincing many men to reenlist and rookie militia volunteers from around the colonies to join the fight. On the way to Princeton, they defeated British soldiers who had received word about the attack in Trenton and were rushing to provide reinforcements. During the battle, Washington is said to have galloped to the front lines. His aides expected him to die in such a dangerous position, but once the musket smoke cleared, he was still on his horse and the Brits had retreated. "It's a fine fox chase, my boys," he shouted, raising his hat.

Washington was a hero after these victories. One journal wrote, "If there are spots on Washington's character, they are like spots on the sun, only discernible by the magnifying powers of a telescope." America was saved from collapse.

The Battle of Germantown

owe and Washington were growing short with each other by October 6, 1777. The two traded letters on that day, each complaining about the behavior of the other's troops. Howe's letter insisted that the Continental army had violated the rules of war by burning the mills of the Loyalists and cutting off their food supply. Washington responded with some gripes of his own, namely the behavior of Howe's troops at Trenton—they "rendered useless" a few mills, he wrote—and he alluded to previous instances in which the British army had committed "wanton and unnecessary depredations," such as the "recent burning of Mills Barnes and Houses at the Head of Elk, and in the vicinity of the Schuylkill." It's understandable that Washington was exasperated in October, because for the past few months, the redcoats had been chasing the Continental army like hounds after a fox. Through New York, New Jersey, and Pennsylvania, the redcoats inched forward and the colonials retreated.

In September 1777, General William Howe had pushed forward on a monthlong campaign, with eighteen thousand British and Hessian soldiers, which began at the northernmost point of the Chesapeake Bay and ended with the capture of Philadelphia. The two climactic battles had been the Battle of Brandywine and a conflict at Paoli. The vicious fighting at Paoli had earned the British and German contingent on that particular campaign an especially gruesome reputation for slaughter. The completion of this campaign culminated on September 26, 1777, when Lord Charles Cornwallis took Philadelphia. The British now ruled the city that had spawned the Declaration of Independence and was considered the American capital, one of the two main cradles of colonial insurrection. When Washington's army lost Brandywine and Paoli, and the British occupied Philadelphia, the American Congress fled to Baltimore.

Having defeated Washington, Howe nevertheless "remained wary of the Americans, who were camped only thirty miles northwest of Philadelphia along Perkiomen Creek between Pennypacker's Mills and Trappe," wrote Germantown historian John B. B. Trussell, Jr. Howe encamped between nine thousand and ten thousand troops, the core of his army, at Germantown, some six miles north of central Philadelphia.

"Germantown itself was a two-mile-long hamlet of stone houses," continued Trussell. "The hilly country, together with the heights along the Wissahickon and the Schuylkill, provided good defensive positions." Howe established a main line of resistance. The western wing was under the Hessian General Wilhelm Knyphausen, who had two battalions. Eastward of Howe were a Hessian brigade and then two British brigades. General James Grant commanded the two British brigades, two corps of dragoons, and an infantry battalion. Closer to Philadelphia there were still more units, squadrons, and battalions. Colonel Thomas Musgrave also commanded a regiment of

This portrait of General William Howe ran in an English publication on May 13, 1786. After the French and Indian War, Howe was feted as a hero in the United States. Yet he also had a host of detractors, in both Britain and the United States, for his failure to bring closure to the Revolutionary War.

infantry. And Howe kept a reserve of two battalions, which could be dispatched where needed.

Washington exercised an ambitious plan of attack, mobilizing his entire army. He organized them into five columns and sent them southward, toward the village of Germantown. His goal was to get through the line of British barracks that stretched east to west across the village in order to march into Philadelphia and reclaim the capital from its British occupiers. The general planned for some of his troops to circle around the British and attack them from the rear. Others would hold the northern position, thereby trapping the redcoats. They were to march for twenty miles overnight in complete silence, so as not to alert the British troops. They set off at dusk on October 3. American General John Armstrong described the situation in a letter to General Horatio Gates a few days after the battle:

> *This disposition appears to have been well made; but to execute such a plan requires great exactness in the officers conducting the columns, as well as punctuality in commencing the march, to bring the whole to the point of action at once; and for this end it is absolutely neces-*

sary that the length and quality of the roads be perfectly ascertained, the time it will take to march them accurately calculated, and guides chosen who are perfectly acquainted with the roads. It is also necessary to assign proper halting-places, either column would arrive before the appointed hour. All these points, I believe, were attended to in the present case; but yet I understood that the guide to the left wing mistook the way, so that, although the right wing halted a considerable time, yet it attacked first, though later than was intended.

The first shots were fired the next morning at five-thirty. The Americans overwhelmed the British, who began to retreat. General Howe, seeing his troops in full flight, shouted, "For shame! For shame! I never saw you retreat before! Form! Form! It's only a scouting party!" One British regiment, led by Musgrave, sought refuge in Cliveden, also known as Chew House, a mansion at the northern end of Germantown Avenue.

"However, [Howe] was soon convinced it was more than a scouting party, as the heads of the enemy's columns soon appeared . . . with three pieces of cannon in their front, [and] immediately fired with grape at the crowd that was standing with General Howe under a large chestnut-tree," wrote British Lieutenant Sir Martin Hunter in his diary, referring to the firing of grapeshot at the British lines.

> *I think I never saw people enjoy a discharge of grape before; but we really all felt pleased to see the enemy make such an appearance, and to hear the grape rattle about the commander-in-chief's ears, after he had accused the battalion of having run away from a scouting party. He rode off immediately, full speed, and we joined the two brigades that were now formed a little way in our rear; but it was not possible for them to make any stand against Washington's whole army, and they all retreated to Germantown, except Colonel Musgrave. . . .*

One hundred and twenty redcoats used the residence as a fort, poking the tips of their muskets out from the second-floor casement windows to fire at the colonials on the front lawn. The rebels shot at the

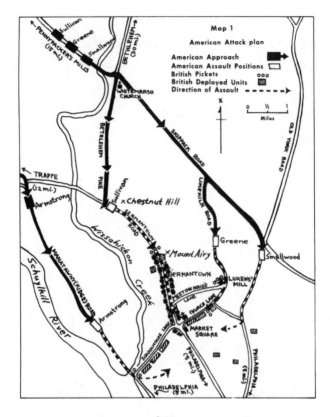

Maps showing Washington's audacious plan. Many military historians, in retrospect, feel it was too complicated and required too much coordination, especially when compounded by weather conditions. While many of Washington's columns engaged the enemy, Chew House was the unforeseen Achilles' heel, being so far behind the front.

(Courtesy Pennsylvania Historical and Museum Commission)

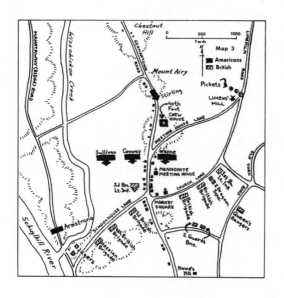

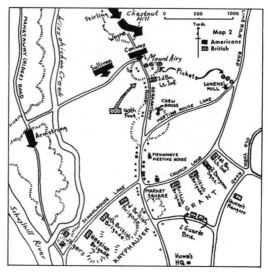

British troops, who were holed up in the house, hidden behind wooden shutters and eighteen-inch-thick granite walls.

The American army still had a lot of fight left, despite the fact that a good number of soldiers were walking around barefoot, their shoes having fallen off in tatters. They were much more disheveled-looking than the redcoats, and decked out in faded greens, blues, browns, and all the different colors of the colonial militias, as opposed to the British, who were in immaculate uniform. Still, the rebels held fast, and a few times, they tried to rush the front door of Clive-den, to no avail.

"This house of Chew's was a strong stone building . . ." wrote Continental Colonel Timothy Pickering in his journal, "having windows on every side, so that you could not approach it without being exposed to a severe fire; which, in fact, was well directed and killed and wounded a great many of our officers and men. Several of our pieces, six-pounders, were brought up within musket-shot of it, and fired round balls at it, but in vain: the enemy, I imagine, were very little hurt; they still kept possession."

Several of the Continentals' columns had bypassed

Cliveden and pressed forward. General Anthony Wayne's men overran several strong holds with another column led by Major General Nathaniel Greene. Both had made strong advancement. There was now confusion in the British ranks.

"At the head of German Town the Continental troops attacked with [vigor], and drove the British who frequently rallied and were drove again and again about the space of two miles," wrote American General John Armstrong. The British soldier Hunter wrote in his diary,

> *General Wayne commanded the advance, and fully expected to be revenged for the surprise we had given him. When the first shots were fired at our pickets, so much had we all Wayne's affair in remembrance that the battalion was out and under arms in a minute. At this time the day had just broke; but it was a very foggy morning and so dark we could not see a hundred yards before us. Just as the battalion had formed, the pickets came in and said the enemy were advancing in force.*
>
> *They had hardly joined the battalion, when*

—— ✳ ——

Chew House Attack, *1777, and* Benjamin Chew House *by Howard Pyle (1898). While the other columns of soldiers sped forward, Chew House (also known as Cliveden) was a thorn in the side of General Henry Knox's light artillery barrages, and the attacks by infantry did little to damage the house. The heavy walls afforded the British an excellent posi-*

tion from which to rain down fire on their opponents. These blasts from well behind the lines caused the leading and until then successful American columns to fall back, believing the British had somehow cut off the rear. Pyle, well known for his illustrated editions of classic stories, rendered the battle with epic sweep.

(Courtesy The Granger Collection, New York)

we heard a loud cry of "Have at the blood-hounds! Revenge Wayne's affair!" and they immediately fired a volley. We gave them one in return, cheered, and charged.

However, confusion also befuddled the Americans. "Already running low on ammunition, hearing the outbreak of heavy firing from the Chew house, and being suddenly attacked from the rear, they believed they were about to be cut off. Their assault, which was on the verge of smashing the British center, came to an abrupt halt, and despite their commander's frantic efforts they began to fall back," Trussell wrote.

Though they lost the battle, the Americans made a respectable showing. For three hours, they had been winning, and this display combined with the American victory at Saratoga two weeks later convinced the French to join in and fight for the American cause.

The battle had revived the sagging spirits of certain colonials. Armstrong wrote to Gates on October 9, 1777.

Every intelligence from town assures us that that the Continental troops in the morning gave the enemy a severe drubbing: Genl. Agnew killed, Grant and Erskin wounded, with some colonels in the hospital and some churches crowded with their wounded. The triumphing Tories again shook at the center, the drooping spirits of the Whigs a little relieved—thus God supports our otherwise sinking spirits which were also animated by your northern success.

Regardless, Washington went on to winter camp, to survive a grueling season of deprivation and cold at Valley Forge, the horrors of which would stay with him and his men for a long time. Meanwhile, Howe wintered in Philadelphia, at the Robert Morris house, an opulent mansion. He availed himself of the festive season in all the best homes of the city, where he was feted and celebrated by many Loyalists.

✳

General Howe's Dog

L ike many battles of the Revolution, Germantown was shrouded in fog. The action started
in the wee hours of the morning and ended
around eight A.M. With the fog, the gunsmoke, the
shouting of the soldiers, the bugle calls, and the drum
signals, the morning was ripe for desertion.

Sure enough, after the Battle of Germantown,
when the American troops marched twenty-five miles
to Pennypacker's Mill in Schwenksville, they discovered a stranger among them. Was it a disoriented soldier? How had he strayed so far from his ranks? It's

possible he had lost his way chasing after a deer or some other animal. The stranger was a Brit, and a diminutive one at that—a little fox terrier, as the lore goes, who had lost his way during the battle and fallen in with the American army as they marched north. The soldiers read the inscription on his collar, which identified him as the property of General William Howe. They brought the pup to the commander in chief's headquarters.

What must Washington's reaction have been? He was a dog lover himself and no doubt would have had empathy for the sadness a man might feel over the loss of a pet. He would have had particular compassion for a fox terrier, because it was a dog he prized for its value during the hunt. Washington himself had many hounds and terriers at Mount Vernon. The pup might have reminded him of his own beloved Sweet Lips, who was miles away in Virginia.

The rules of war stated that soldiers could be taken prisoner but that a man's personal property should be returned. A year earlier, Washington's men had found the personal letters of a British officer left behind at an encampment. After scanning them for military secrets, Washington had returned these letters to

Howe with a note requesting that they be given to the officer whose name they bore. There must have been some indiscretion revealed in the letters, because Washington asked Howe not to read the contents. According to a return note Howe wrote to Washington, he did as his adversary asked and delivered the letters without peeking.

One of Washington's officers suggested keeping the little dog as a mascot, but the general demurred. He opted to return him to his rightful owner, but not before wiping him clean, brushing his fur, and giving him food. He asked aide-de-camp Alexander Hamilton to pen the note to Howe. The note read, "General Washington's compliments to General Howe, does himself the pleasure to return him a Dog, which accidentally fell into his hands, and by the inscription on the collar, appears to belong to General Howe." Washington sent one of his men as an envoy, to backtrack the twenty-five miles to Germantown, where Howe was headquartered at an estate called Stenton.

The American soldier carried in one hand the dog and in the other a white flag of truce, so that the British would know he was approaching unarmed, and on a peaceful mission. It's possible that he passed

Washington's note to Howe.

(Courtesy Library of Congress, Manuscript Division)

British soldiers who wondered what this colonial was doing in enemy territory, holding a flag and a little dog. They might have laughed or pointed or joked about the American soldier and his terrier. One of Howe's officers described the return:

> *The General seemed most pleased at the return of the dog. He took him upon his lap, seemingly uncaring that the mud from the dog's feet soiled his tunic. Whilst he stroked the dog, he discovered a tightly folded message that had been secreted under the dog's wide collar. The General read the message, which seemed to have a good effect upon him. Although I know not what it said, it is likely to have been penned by the commander of the rebellion.*

There's no record of what this second note said, and Sir William's response is gone with the rest of his papers, but presumably, he wouldn't have let the return of a lost dog pass without some acknowledgment. We know that he appreciated the gesture, since he later referred to the incident as "an honorable act of a gentleman."

Joseph Ellis has a different interpretation. He notes that Washington tried "to exaggerate the American achievement [at Germantown] and, in effect, claimed victory. He even adopted the posture of the victorious commander toward Howe, making a point of returning Howe's dog, which he had found wandering the battle field searching for his master."

Why did George Washington go to all this trouble to return a dog? For one thing, it was a manner of civility. Number 110 in *Rules of Civility* reads, "Labour to keep alive in your Breast that Little Spark of Ce[les]tial fire Called Conscience." And in *Morals*, Seneca advises, "An honest man can never be outdone in courtesy." In at least one earlier instance, Washington opted *not* to reunite a dog with its owner, when one of his third-ranking generals, Charles Lee, was captured by the British while in the company of a prostitute at a tavern near New York in December 1776. Lee was known for his love of his dogs—he always traveled with at least two. Being held prisoner in New York, he was dogless, and determined to do something about it. He wrote a letter to Washington, asking the commander in chief to negotiate some kind of deal with the British that would result in them letting him maintain a dog in captivity. Washington wrote back to Lee, telling him that he was sorry Lee was deprived of the friendship and amusement of his pets but that he would do nothing. As far as Washington was concerned, Lee's dogs were safer in Virginia.

Judging from his reactions, Lee must have been incensed. At the end of March, he divulged military secrets to General Howe in return for arranging for his dogs to be shipped up to him in New York. Apparently his plan didn't work, because Lee was released, still dogless, in May. The general's traitorous activities didn't become public until well after his death, so he did not receive the Benedict Arnold treatment, although he certainly deserved it.

Washington might have known that Lee was immoral at heart. Maybe that's part of the reason he opted not to help reunite his colleague with his dogs. If we analyze the behavior of the two men from Washington's point of view, Howe seems much more deserving than Lee of the company of such a noble and loyal creature as a dog. It's also possible that Washington was sending a statement about Americans by returning the dog—he may have been trying to show that the colonials were just as gentlemanly and mannerly as loyal English subjects. They would do fine on their own, without the guidance and imprimatur of the monarchy. Or, his decision to return the dog could have been an attempt to inject a little levity into a gruesome war.

※

The War Ends

Howe resigned from his post soon after his dog was returned. His letter of resignation, dated October 22, 1777, reads, "I am led to hope that I may be relieved from this very painful service, wherein I have not the good fortune to enjoy the necessary confidence and support of my superiors. . . ." He had abandoned hope that the conflict might be resolved peacefully, and after his letter was penned and sent, he devoted himself to having a good time in Philadelphia during the winter of 1778. The city was rich with taverns. Some, like The Pewter Platter and The Crooked Billet, were named for the objects that hung above their front doors. Others were named for livestock, like The Bull's Head, and other animals: The Bear, The Rattlesnake. The Loyalists who were left in Philadelphia at the time of the British occupation probably hung their hats at the more imperial-minded establishments, like The Queen's Head, The King of Prussia, and The King of Poland, but the officers frequented house parties and luxurious establishments like The City Tavern, a restaurant and inn built in 1773 in "the latest London mode." During the British occupation, many colorful balls and banquets were held here. Howe was wined and dined by Philadelphia Loyalists, accompanied all the while by Mrs. Loring, the "First Lady of the British army." There were weekly balls, suppers, music parties, and plays.

On February 4, Sir William received word that His Majesty had relieved him of duty and that Sir Henry Clinton would take charge. Howe prepared to leave. The general's good-bye party was legendary. His officers, who had served with him from Bunker Hill to Brandywine, planned a day of festivities, the immortal *mischianza*, of May 18, 1778. The pageant began with an elaborate procession down the Delaware River, with men dressed as knights and women as Turkish maidens. The grand march continued ashore as the revelers proceeded through an avenue of knights and ended up at a Loyalist's mansion, where they danced, watched a fireworks display, and feasted in a hall that had been built for the occasion. The guests were served by twenty-four slaves in Asian dress with silver collars and bracelets. The opulence of the gala showed how popular Howe had been with his men, how sad they were to see him go—and perhaps how badly they needed to let off steam.

Howe sailed back to England a week later on the *Andromeda*.

✳

When the war ended, in 1783, after the American victory at the Battle of Yorktown, George Washington could have seized power and made himself king. The year before, while official peace talks were in progress, Washington was approached by an officer named Lewis Nicola, who asked him to join an armed rebellion against Congress and allow himself to be set up as king. But Nicola simply did not understand George

Washington's character. "You could not have found a person to whom your schemes are more disagreeable," Washington replied. "If you have any regard for your Country, concern for yourself or posterity, or respect for me, to banish these thoughts from your Mind, and never communicate, as from yourself, or any one else, a sentiment of the like Nature."

The British assumed that Washington would now become king of America. When King George heard of Washington's plans to give up his commission, he shook visibly and said, "If he does that, he is the greatest man alive." So he was. Washington surrendered his sword to Congress. As historian Gary Willis has written, Washington "gained power by his willingness to give it up." He returned to Mount Vernon and his life as a gentleman farmer, at least until he was elected president in 1789, after which he ran the farm indirectly through regular missives to his chief overseer. For now though, he took obvious delight in returning to his land. On February 1, 1784, he wrote to his good friend the Marquis de Lafayette, "At length my Dear Marquis I am become a private citizen on the banks of the Potomac, and under the shadow of my own Vine and my own Fig-tree. . . ." His diaries from this time consist of detailed weather records, agricultural notations, the chronicling of a constant rotation of dinner guests, daily rounds of his estate on horseback, and records of animal husbandry.

Even in 1785, when he was fifty-three, Washington was still quite the adventurous horseman. The Marquis de Chastellux visited Mount Vernon in that year, and later wrote of one of the general's horses, "He is as good as he is handsome . . ." and of Washington, "It is the General who himself breaks all his own horses; and he is a very excellent and bold horseman, leaping the highest fences, and going extremely quick, without standing upon his stirrups, bearing on the bridle, or letting his horse run wild."

As historian and biographer James Thomas Flexner noted of Washington's preoccupations in the years after the war, "He was still much concerned with the breeding of horses and hounds, with races and hunts."

Although while making their daily rounds the general and his hounds "frequently raised a fox, Washington often noted in his diary, 'catch'd nothing.'" Still, hunting was one of his favorite pastimes.

When Washington's former aide-de-camp David

✳

Washington greeting his family at Mount Vernon after returning from hunting.

Humphreys wrote his reminiscences of General Washington, they in effect became the only biography of his life Washington ever commented on. Humphreys wrote, "He keeps a pack of hounds, and in the season indulges himself with hunting once in a week, at which diversion the Gentlemen of Alexandria often assist." Washington was compelled to comment on this aside, making the note, "Once a week is his fixed hunts though sometimes he goes oftener."

Daily trials and tribulations at Mount Vernon included foxes and wolves who picked off Washington's prized sheep as steadily as some of the redcoats had picked off his men in the early days of the Revolution. Like the rest of his livestock, Washington's sheep were descended from the finest bloodlines in Europe. Their coats provided wool for homespun clothes, and their bulk provided cheese, mutton, and lamb for George and Martha's frequent dinner parties. The sheep were not meant for the maws of mangy foxes, wolves, and stray dogs who roamed Virginia, and Washington set out to do something to stop the killing.

In 1787 he wrote to the Marquis de Lafayette for help in finding some "true Irish wolf dogs" or some of the same Irish greyhounds the conquistadors had used to hunt Native Americans in the Caribbean and in Central and South America. Lafayette tried but found none. An Irish gentleman named Sir Edward Newenham also tried to help. "I have been these several years endeavoring to get that breed without success," he wrote Washington. "It is nearly annihilated. I have heard of a bitch in northern Ireland but not of a couple anywhere."

Washington gave up on finding dogs to hunt his sheeps' marauders. Instead, he instructed his farm manager to destroy any sheep-killing animal as well as any dog who didn't seem to belong to anyone or to be serving any specific purpose. All unassigned beasts were fair game. He also forbade his slaves to have dogs, as he was afraid they might use them for stealing.

The Marquis de Lafayette did come through on an earlier request of Washington's for some French hounds, even though French hounds were particularly hard to come by in the mid-1780s. The French monarch of that time considered English hounds superior, and since all the nobles followed their king's lead, English hounds were much easier to find than their Gallic counterparts. Still, Lafayette managed to acquire seven French hounds—three males and four

Mount Vernon was originally bequeathed to Lawrence Washington, George's older half brother, but upon his death in 1754 the five-hundred-acre Mansion House Farm, as it was known then, was passed on to George. He added on to the original house and expanded the grounds. In Washington's time, the Mount Vernon plantation came to encompass five farms and eight thousand acres. Each farm was a complete unit, with its own buildings, equipment, livestock, overseers, and slaves.

females—from a Comte d'Oilliamson. He sent them to America under the care of eighteen-year-old John Quincy Adams, who was returning home in the summer of 1785 after an extended European tour to attend Harvard in the fall.

All summer, Washington anticipated the arrival of Lafayette's hounds, and when he had heard nothing by late August, he mentioned the matter in an August 22 letter to William Grayson, his assistant and an aide-de-camp during the Revolution. He asked Grayson whether he'd heard Adams say anything about the hounds. "It would have been civil in the young Gentleman to have dropped me a line respecting the disposal of them," Washington wrote, "especially as war is declared on the canine species in New York, and they being strangers, and not having formed alliances for self-defence, but on the contrary, distressed and friendless may also have been exposed not only to war, but to pestilence and famine also."

The "war" to which Washington alluded in his letter was made official on October 26, 1785, when the Common Council of New York City passed an ordinance "for guarding against the mischief which may arise from distempered or Mad Dogs," mandating that dogs be

chained, leashed, muzzled, or confined, or face arrest—
and death if not bailed out by their owners. The ordinance was a response to the growing population of
strays and pets in the city. Packs of strays roamed the
streets, fighting with one another, attacking pedestrians
and horses, and stealing food from street vendors. New
Yorkers used the dogs as a source of cheap entertain-
ment, throwing them into pits to see which could kill the
most rats in the shortest amount of time. Others picked
the dogs off the street and put them to work turning
spits and grinders or pumping bellows for blacksmiths.
The dogs that weren't put to use often seemed mad and
distempered, especially during the hot summer months,
even if they didn't technically have rabies. As there was
no vaccine for rabies, the city protected its human
inhabitants by killing the sick-looking dogs.

Of course, Lafayette's pure hounds were not likely
to be mistaken for rabid strays. Still, young Adams, a
future president of the United States, didn't seem particularly fond of the animals. He passed them off to
Dr. John Cochran upon his arrival in New York, with
nary a word to Washington. Cochran, the chief army
physician and surgeon under Washington during the
Revolution, immediately found a place for the hounds

THE RIGHT HONOURABLE

The MARQUIS DE LA FAYETTE,

Unanimously chosen Commandant General of the National Guards.

The brave FAYETTE, of late in foreign climes unfurl'd
The *Gallic* flag – and fought, to liberate a world :
Today, inspir'd by him, France breathes the godlike flame ;
And millions, rang'd beneath his standard–FREEDOM claims

Translated from the French of the Chev. Fdr. Iarminelli

Marie-Joseph-Paul-Yves-Roch-Gilbert du Motier, Marquis de Lafayette, was born in 1757. Before his second birthday, his father, a colonel in the grenadiers, was killed at Minden. Lafayette's real introduction to America came at a dinner on August 8, 1775, when the young marquis came into contact with the Duke of Gloucester, who spoke with sympathy of the struggle going on in the colonies. Eventually, Lafayette landed near Charleston, South Carolina, on June 13, 1777, and when the leaders of the Revolution learned of his mission they welcomed him with open arms. He was not even twenty years old! Later that summer, he met General Washington, and a friendship developed between the two that lasted until Washington's death. Lafayette would never forget the great American.

The Marquis de Lafayette served as a member of Washington's staff, and fought alongside him at the Battle of the Brandywine, where he was wounded. In December 1777, he went with Washington and the Revolutionary army to winter quarters at Valley Forge. This period engraving includes four lines of verse "translated from the French of the Chev. P. de Berainville" beneath his image.

*In 1780, Lafayette's relentless lobbying of the French govern-
ment resulted in French troops being sent to aid Washington.
Lafayette set sail for France from Boston on the United States
ship* Alliance *on December 23, but beforehand he wrote to
Washington, saying: "Adieu, my dear General; I know your
heart so well that I am sure that no distance can alter your
attachment to me. With the same candour I assure that my
love, respect, my gratitude for you, are above expression; that,
at the moment of leaving you, I felt more than ever the
strength of those friendly ties that forever bind me to you."
Lafayette paid his celebrated visit to Mount Vernon in 1784;
this engraving depicts his departure. He later sent Washington
one of the keys to the Bastille.*

--- ✳ ---

The breed depicted here is the original Bleu de Gascogne, and it is probably closest in type and size to ancient hounds. The Grand Bleu de Gascogne, thought to be one of the world's largest scent hounds, was first imported during early colonial days by French settlers, and Washington was presented with seven of them by Lafayette in 1785. The Grand Bleu was used for hunting deer, boar, and wolf in France, and was famed for its ability to "cold-trail"—that is, to find and follow trails as much as three days old. While relatively slow moving, the breed was renowned for its stamina and scenting ability. Later, as larger game disappeared in France, the smaller Petit Bleu de Gascogne was developed.

on a boat headed for Virginia. They arrived at Mount Vernon on August 31.

The very next day, Washington wrote to Lafayette. (Young John Adams could have learned a thing or two about communication from Washington.) "The Hounds which you were so obliging as to send me arrived safe," Washington wrote, "and are of promising appearance; to Monsieur le Compte Doilliamson (if I miscall him, your handwriting is to blame, and in honor you are bound to rectify the error); and in an *especial* manner to his fair Comptesse, my thanks are due for this favor: the enclosed letter which I give you the trouble of forwarding contains my acknowledgement of their obliging attention to me on this occasion."

Lafayette had told Washington of Countess d'Oilliamson's fondness for one of the female hounds. In his letter to d'Oilliamson, Washington assured the count that the hound his wife had favored would receive special treatment at Mount Vernon:

> *Sir: I have just received seven very fine Hounds,*
> *for which, the Marqs. de la Fayette informs me,*
> *I am indebted to your goodness. I know not in*
> *what terms to acknowledge my gratitude for the*

obligation, but pray you to be assured that I have a due sense of the honor; and feel in a particular manner the force of the goodness of Madame la Comptesse, to whom the Marqs. adds, I am beholden for a favorite *hound. I pray you to offer my best respects, and to make my acknowledgment of this favor, acceptable to her: at the same time I beg you to assure her that her favorite shall not suffer under my care, but become the object of my particular attention.*

Washington happily incorporated the French hounds into his and Martha's life at Mount Vernon. Paintings from the time show that Washington's hunting dogs had the run of the kitchen. Martha couldn't have been too happy when Vulcan, one of Lafayette's hounds, tore into the dining room and stole a freshly cooked Virginia ham from the dinner table. It was written that he ran "straight to the kennel with it locked in his great jaws." Washington crossed these large, French hounds with his own smaller Virginia hounds in search of the perfect hunting dog. In his diaries, he wrote that he wanted to create "a superior dog, one that had speed, scent and brains."

A diary entry from the year 1786 is a mere sampling of Washington's longtime hobby and obsession. On February 18, Washington entered the following in his journal:

> *Saturday 18th. Thermometer at 45 in the Morning—56 at Noon and 50 at Night.*
>
> *The morning lowered—cleard at Noon and about two it rained a little; with appearances of a good deal, at first—however it soon ceased, though it continued cloudy till night, when the Wind, which had blowed pretty fresh from the Southward all day, shifted to the No. West.*
>
> *Began the yards back of the Green house designed for the Jack Ass & Magnolia.*
>
> *The Bitch Stately was lined by the Dog Vulcan. Jupiter had been put to her and Venus but never seemed to take the least notice of them but whether he ever lined either of them is not certain. The contrary is supposed.*

Washington's experiments in breeding were cut short when he traveled to Philadelphia in 1787 to chair the Continental Congress, which was busy creat-

--- ✳ ---

The fireplace in the kitchen at Mount Vernon. It was from the kitchen table that one of Washington's favorite hounds, Vulcan, stole a ham and dashed off with it. Although the ham was recovered, it was inedible. And while Martha was quite vexed by the episode, the general found it hilarious.

ing the new country's government. Of course, he couldn't leave everything at home in Virginia. Washington brought some of his hounds with him when he was inaugurated as the first president of the United States in April 1789. His time as president were spent in the American capitals of New York (during his first term), and Philadelphia (during his second).

In the fall of 1790, the new American government settled into Philadelphia. Thomas Jefferson, John Adams, and the rest moved into houses in and around the city, ready to take on the task of governing the new country. As David McCullough, author of *John Adams*, noted, "Washington arrived and moved into the Robert Morris house on Market Street, considered the grandest residence in Philadelphia. (General Sir William Howe had made it his headquarters during the occupation.)"

That year, Washington went home to Mount Vernon for Christmas. "He stopped by the stable each day, where he offered a handful of grain to Nelson, his old warhorse from Yorktown." But no hunting was noted.

Washington set a precedent for presidents owning pets. To this day, more animals than people have lived

Early-twentieth-century photograph of the library at Mount Vernon. It was here that Washington kept careful records of his agricultural endeavors and recorded his thoughts in a daily diary. He also devoted many hours here to planning the breeding of his horses and hounds.

(Courtesy Library of Congress)

in the White House. During Washington's time in office, he kept horses and hounds: Mopsey, Cloe, Forester, Captain, Lady Rover, good old Sweet Lips, Scentwell, and Searcher. A few of these hounds were from the shipment Lafayette sent over from France.

Presidents' pets have mostly been dogs, with the odd cat or guinea pig thrown in here and there. Our nation's thirtieth president, Calvin Coolidge, went so far as to suggest that being a dog person was part of the job description of chief executive. "Any man who does not like dogs and want them about," he famously stated, "does not deserve to be in the White House." Though there's no doubt these men were all very fond of their pets, it also doesn't hurt a president's image to be publicly enamored of a small, furry animal. Dogs are the great equalizer. Seeing the commander in chief in the company of a dog certainly goes far to humanize him in the eyes of voters, fellow politicians, and world leaders. Warren Harding posed in a campaign poster with his Airedale, Laddie Boy, above the slogan BACK TO NORMALCY WITH HARDING. It's entirely normal for a man to have a dog as his best friend, but how normal is it that Laddie Boy was given his own hand-carved, high-backed chair to sit in during cabinet

---- ✳ ----

A portrait of George Washington, painted by Gilbert Stuart. Certainly, Stuart chose to depict Washington as a man of gravitas, importance, and restraint.

meetings, and his own servant, whose official title was Master of the White House Hounds?

Other presidents took their dogs along on official business. Franklin Delano Roosevelt's Scottie, Fala, went everywhere with his master. He rode in FDR's limo and even went on diplomatic missions overseas. He was trained to shake hands with visiting dignitaries and to stand at attention on his hind legs when "The Star-Spangled Banner" was played. Gerald Ford made use of his golden retriever, Liberty, to break up Oval Office meetings when he felt they were going too long. He'd whistle for her, and she'd bound into the office and up onto the laps of visitors who'd worn out their welcome.

There are no such anecdotes of Washington's dogs during his presidential years. And after he gave his farewell speech in September 1796, he enjoyed fewer than three years of retirement at Mount Vernon. On December 14, 1799, at age sixty-eight, he died of a throat infection.

Washington was outlived by William Howe, who passed away in 1814 at age eighty-five. When Howe returned to England directly after the war, he had much to explain to Parliament. Other officers had tat-

※

A picture of George and Martha at Mount Vernon executed sometime after the war. While the children are not identified, it is known that two of Martha's grandchildren came to live with the Washingtons then, and many of her grandchildren regularly came to stay. More often than not, the house had quite a number of guests staying at any one time.

tled about his inaction, and he was asked to defend himself. Though he offered tactical explanations for each enigmatic move, his explanations were ambiguous enough to leave historians wondering whether Howe's heart was ever really in the war. And it's worth wondering, too, whether the general would have resigned from duty so soon after the Battle of Germantown if General Washington hadn't returned his dog. The noble gesture may have reinforced for Howe what he felt so strongly even before the war began: that these colonials' rights were as inalienable as his own.

✳

Rules of Civility & Decent Behaviour in Company and Conversation Ferry Farm, c. 1744

1st   Every Action done in Company, ought to be with Some Sign of Respect, to those that are Present.

2d   When in Company, put not your Hands to any Part of the Body, not usualy Discovered.

3d   Shew Nothing to your Freind that may affright him.

4th   In the Presence of Others Sing not to yourself with a humming Noise, nor Drum with your Fingers or Feet.

5th   If You Cough, Sneeze, Sigh, or Yawn, do it not
Loud but Privately; and Speak not in your Yawning,
but put Your handkercheif or Hand before your face
and turn aside.

6th   Sleep not when others Speak, Sit not when others stand, Speak not when you Should hold your
Peace, walk not on when others Stop.

7th   Put not off your Cloths in the presence of Others, nor go out your Chamber half Drest.

8th   At Play and at Fire its Good manners to Give
Place to the last Commer, and affect not to Speak
Louder than Ordinary.

9th   Spit not in the Fire, nor Stoop low before it neither Put your Hands into the Flames to warm them,
nor Set your Feet upon the Fire especially if there be
meat before it.

10th   When you Sit down, Keep your Feet firm and
Even, without putting one on the other or Crossing
them.

11th   Shift not yourself in the Sight of others nor Gnaw your nails.

12th   Shake not the head, Feet, or Legs rowl not the Eys lift not one eyebrow higher than the other wry not the mouth, and bedew no mans face with your Spittle, by appr[oaching too nea]r him [when] you Speak.

13th   Kill no Vermin as Fleas, lice ticks &c in the Sight of Others, if you See any filth or thick Spittle put your foot Dexteriously upon it if it be upon the Cloths of your Companions, Put it off privately, and if it be upon your own Cloths return Thanks to him who puts it off.

14th   Turn not your Back to others especially in Speaking, Jog not the Table or Desk on which Another reads or writes, lean not upon any one.

15th   Keep your Nails clean and Short, also your Hands and Teeth Clean yet without Shewing any great Concern for them.

16th   Do not Puff up the Cheeks, Loll not out the tongue rub the Hands, or beard, thrust out the lips, or bite them or keep the Lips too open or too Close.

17th   Be no Flatterer, neither Play with any that delights not to be Play'd Withal.

18th   Read no Letters, Books, or Papers in Company but when there is a Necessity for the doing of it you must ask leave: come not near the Books or Writings of Another so as to read them unless desired or give your opinion of them unask'd also look not nigh when another is writing a Letter.

19th   let your Countenance be pleasant but in Serious Matters Somewhat grave.

20th   The Gestures of the Body must be Suited to the discourse you are upon.

21st   Reproach none for the Infirmaties of Nature, nor Delight to Put them that have in mind thereof.

22d   Shew not yourself glad at the Misfortune of another though he were your enemy.

23d   When you see a Crime punished, you may be inwardly Pleased; but always shew Pity to the Suffering Offender.

[24th   Do not laugh too loud or] too much at any Publick [Spectacle].

25th   Superfluous Complements and all Affectation of Ceremonie are to be avoided, yet where due they are not to be Neglected.

26th   In Pulling off your Hat to Persons of Distinction, as Noblemen, Justices, Churchmen &c make a Reverence, bowing more or less according to the Custom of the Better Bred, and Quality of the Person. Amongst your equals expect not always that they Should begin with you first, but to Pull off the Hat when there is no need is Affectation, in the Manner of Saluting and resaluting in words keep to the most usual Custom.

27th   Tis ill manners to bid one more eminent than yourself be covered as well as not to do it to whom it's due Likewise he that makes too much haste to Put on his hat does not well, yet he ought to Put it on at the first, or at most the Second time of being ask'd; now what is herein Spoken, of Qualification in behaviour in Saluting, ought also to be observed in taking of Place, and Sitting down for ceremonies without Bounds is troublesome.

28th   If any one come to Speak to you while you are are Sitting Stand up tho he be your Inferiour, and when you Present Seats let it be to every one according to his Degree.

29th   When you meet with one of Greater Quality than yourself, Stop, and retire especially if it be at a Door or any Straight place to give way for him to Pass.

30th   In walking the highest Place in most Countrys Seems to be on the right hand therefore Place yourself on the left of him whom you desire to Honour: but if three walk together the mid[dest] Place is the most

Honourable the wall is usually given to the most worthy if two walk together.

31st   If any one far Surpassess others, either in age,
Estate, or Merit [yet] would give Place to a meaner than
hims[elf in his own lodging or elsewhere] the one ought
not to except it, S[o he on the other part should not use
much earnestness nor offer] it above once or twice.

32d   To one that is your equal, or not much inferior
you are to give the cheif Place in your Lodging and he
to who 'tis offered ought at the first to refuse it but at
the Second to accept though not without acknowledg-
ing his own unworthiness.

33d   They that are in Dignity or in office have in all
places Preceedency but whilst they are Young they
ought to respect those that are their equals in Birth or
other Qualitys, though they have no Publick charge.

34th   It is good Manners to prefer them to whom we
Speak befo[re] ourselves especially if they be above us
with whom in no Sort we ought to begin.

35th   Let your Discourse with Men of Business be Short and Comprehensive.

36th   Artificers & Persons of low Degree ought not to use many ceremonies to Lords, or Others of high Degree but Respect and high[ly] Honour them, and those of high Degree ought to treat them with affibility & Courtesie, without Arrogancy.

37th   In Speaking to men of Quality do not lean nor Look them full in the Face, nor approach too near them at lest Keep a full Pace from them.

38th   In visiting the Sick, do not Presently play the Physicion if you be not Knowing therein.

39th   In writing or Speaking, give to every Person his due Title According to his Degree & the Custom of the Place.

40th   Strive not with your Superiers in argument, but always Submit your Judgment to others with Modesty.

41st Undertake not to Teach your equal in the art himself Proffesses; it Savours of arrogancy.

42d Let thy ceremonies in] Courtesie be proper to the Dignity of his place [with whom thou conversest for it is absurd to ac]t the same with a Clown and a Prince.

43d Do not express Joy before one sick or in pain for that contrary Passion will aggravate his Misery.

44th When a man does all he can though it Succeeds not well blame not him that did it.

45th Being to advise or reprehend any one, consider whether it ought to be in publick or in Private; presently, or at Some other time in what terms to do it & in reproving Shew no Sign of Cholar but do it with all Sweetness and Mildness.

46th Take all Admonitions thankfully in what Time or Place Soever given but afterwards not being culpable take a Time [&] Place convenient to let him him know it that gave them.

[4]7th   Mock not nor Jest at any thing of Impor-
tance break [n]o Jest that are Sharp Biting and if you
Deliver any thing witty and Pleasent abtain from
Laughing thereat yourself.

48th   Wherein wherein you reprove Another be
unblameable yourself; for example is more prevalent
than Precepts.

[4]9   Use no Reproachfull Language against any one
neither Curse nor Revile.

[5]0th   Be not hasty to beleive flying Reports to the
Disparag[e]ment of any.

51st   Wear not your Cloths, foul, unript or Dusty but
See they be Brush'd once every day at least and take
heed tha[t] you approach not to any Uncleaness.

52d   In your Apparel be Modest and endeavour to
accomodate Nature, rather than to procure Admira-
tion keep to the Fashio[n] of your equals Such as are
Civil and orderly with respect to Times and Places.

53d   Run not in the Streets, neither go t[oo s]lowly nor wit[h] Mouth open go not Shaking yr Arms [kick not the earth with yr feet, go] not upon the Toes, nor in a Dancing [fashion].

54th   Play not the Peacock, looking every where about you, to See if you be well Deck't, if your Shoes fit well if your Stokings sit neatly, and Cloths handsomely.

55th   Eat not in the Streets, nor in the House, out of Season.

56th   Associate yourself with Men of good Quality if you Esteem your own Reputation; for 'tis better to be alone than in bad Company.

57th   In walking up and Down in a House, only with One in Compan[y] if he be Greater than yourself, at the first give him the Right hand and Stop not till he does and be not the first that turns, and when you do turn let it be with your face towards him, if he be a Man of Great Quality, walk not with him Cheek by Joul but Somewhat behind him; but yet in Such a Manner that he may easily Speak to you.

58th   Let your Conversation be without Malice or Envy, for 'tis a Sig[n o]f a Tractable and Commendable Nature: And in all Causes of Passion [ad]mit Reason to Govern.

59th   Never express anything unbecoming, nor Act agst the Rules Mora[l] before your inferiours.

60th   Be not immodest in urging your Freinds to Discover a Secret.

61st   Utter not base and frivilous things amongst grave and Learn'd Men nor very Difficult Questians or Subjects, among the Ignorant or things hard to be believed, Stuff not your Discourse with Sentences amongst your Betters nor Equals.

62d   Speak not of doleful Things in a Time of Mirth or at the Table; Speak not of Melancholy Things as Death and Wounds, and if others Mention them Change if you can the Discourse tell not your Dreams, but to your intimate Friend.

63d   A Man o[ug]ht not to value himself of his Atchievements, or rare Qua[lities of wit; much less of his rich]es Virtue or Kindred.

64th   Break not a Jest where none take pleasure in mirth Laugh not aloud, nor at all without Occasion, deride no mans Misfortune, tho' there Seem to be Some cause.

65th   Speak not injurious Words neither in Jest nor Earnest Scoff at none although they give Occasion.

66th   Be not froward but friendly and Courteous; the first to Salute hear and answer & be not Pensive when it's a time to Converse.

67th   Detract not from others neither be excessive in Commanding.

68th   Go not thither, where you know not, whether you Shall be Welcome or not. Give not Advice with[out] being Ask'd & when desired [d]o it briefly.

[6]9   If two contend together take not the part of either unconstrain[ed]; and be not obstinate in your own Opinion, in Things indiferent be of the Major Side.

70th   Reprehend not the imperfections of others for that belong[s] to Parents Masters and Superiours.

71st   Gaze not on the marks or blemishes of Others and ask not how they came. What you may Speak in Secret to your Friend deliver not before others.

72d   Speak not in an unknown Tongue in Company but in your own Language and that as those of Quality do and not as the Vulgar; Sublime matters treat Seriously.

73d   Think before you Speak pronounce not imperfectly nor bring ou[t] your Words too hastily but orderly & distinctly.

74th   When Another Speaks be attentive your Self and disturb not the Audience if any hesitate in his Words help him not nor Prompt him without desired,

Interrupt him not, nor Answer him till his Speec[h] be ended.

75th   In the midst of Discourse ask [not of what one treateth] but if you Perceive any Stop because of [your coming you may well intreat him gently] to Proceed: If a Person of Quality comes in while your Conversing it's handsome to Repeat what was said before.

76th   While you are talking, Point not with your Finger at him of Whom you Discourse nor Approach too near him to whom you talk especially to his face.

77th   Treat with men at fit Times about Business & Whisper not in the Company of Others.

78th   Make no Comparisons and if any of the Company be Commended for any brave act of Vertue, commend not another for the Same.

79th   Be not apt to relate News if you know not the truth thereof. In Discoursing of things you Have heard Name not your Author always A [Se]cret Discover not.

80th   Be not Tedious in Discourse or in reading unless you find the Company pleased therewith.

81st   Be not Curious to Know the Affairs of Others neither approach those that Speak in Private.

82d   Undertake not what you cannot Perform but be Carefull to keep your Promise.

83d   When you deliver a matter do it without Passion & with Discretion, howev[er] mean the Person be you do it too.

84th   When your Superiours talk to any Body hearken not neither Speak nor Laugh.

85th   In Company of these of Higher Quality than yourself Speak not ti[l] you are ask'd a Question then Stand upright put of your Hat & Answer in few words.

86   In Disputes, be not So Desireous to Overcome as not to give Liberty to each one to deliver his Opinion and Submit to the Judgment of the Major Part especially if they are Judges of the Dispute.

[87th Let thy carriage be such] as becomes a Man
Grave Settled and attentive [to that which is spoken.
Contra]dict not at every turn what others Say.

88th Be not tedious in Discourse, make not many
Digressigns, nor rep[eat] often the Same manner of
Discourse.

89th Speak not Evil of the absent for it is unjust.

90 Being Set at meat Scratch not neither Spit Cough
or blow your Nose except there's a Necessity for it.

91st Make no Shew of taking great Delight in your
Victuals, Feed no[t] with Greediness; cut your Bread
with a Knife, lean not on the Table neither find fault
with what you Eat.

92 Take no Salt or cut Bread with your Knife
Greasy.

93 Entertaining any one at table it is decent to present him wt. meat, Undertake not to help others unde-
sired by the Master.

[9]4th   If you Soak bread in the Sauce let it be no more than what you [pu]t in your Mouth at a time and blow not your broth at Table [bu]t Stay till Cools of it Self.

[95]th   Put not your meat to your Mouth with your Knife in your ha[nd ne]ither Spit forth the Stones of any fruit Pye upon a Dish nor Cas[t an]ything under the table.

[9]6   It's unbecoming to Stoop much to ones Meat Keep your Fingers clea[n &] when foul wipe them on a Corner of your Table Napkin.

[97]th   Put not another bit into your Mouth til the former be Swallowed [l]et not your Morsels be too big for the Gowls.

98th   Drink not nor talk with your mouth full neither Gaze about you while you are a Drinking.

99th   Drink not too leisurely nor yet too hastily. Before and after Drinking wipe your Lips breath not then or Ever with too Great a Noise, for its uncivil.

100   Cleanse not your teeth with the Table Cloth Napkin Fork or Knife but if Others do it let it be done wt. a Pick Tooth.

101st   Rince not your Mouth in the Presence of Others.

102d   It is out of use to call upon the Company often to Eat nor need you Drink to others every Time you Drink.

103d   In Company of your Betters be no[t longer in eating] than they are lay not your Arm but o[nly your hand upon the table].

104th   It belongs to the Chiefest in Company to unfold his Napkin and fall to Meat first, But he ought then to Begin in time & to Dispatch [w]ith Dexterity that the Slowest may have time allowed him.

[1]05th   Be not Angry at Table whatever happens & if you have reason to be so, Shew it not but on a Chearfull Countenance especially if there be Strangers for Good Humour makes one Dish of Meat a Feas[t].

[1]06th Set not yourself at the upper of the Table but if it Be your Due or that the Master of the house will have it So, Contend not, least you Should Trouble the Company.

107th If others talk at Table be attentive but talk not with Meat in your Mouth.

108th When you Speak of God or his Atributes, let it be Seriously & [wt.] Reverence. Honour & Obey your Natural Parents altho they be Poor.

109th Let your Recreations be Manfull not Sinfull.

110th Labour to keep alive in your Breast that Little Spark of Ce[les]tial fire Called Conscience.

❋

Breed Standard of the Treeing Walker

(Reprinted by permission of the
United Kennel Club)

HISTORY

The Treeing Walker was developed from certain strains of English Walker Foxhounds. The credit for the development of the Walker Foxhound goes to two men—George Washington Maupin and John W. Walker. Both men were from Kentucky. Before that time, Thomas Walker of Albemarle County, Virginia, imported hounds from England in 1742. George Washington, who was an avid fox hunter, also imported several hounds from England in 1770. These dogs became the foundation strains of the Virginia

Hounds, which were developed into the Walker hound.

At least one major out cross was made in the 19th century that was to forever influence the breed. Strangely, the out cross was with a stolen dog from Tennessee of unknown origin, known as Tennessee Lead. Lead didn't look like the Virginia strain of English Foxhounds of that day. But he had an exceptional amount of game sense, plenty of drive and speed and a clear, short mouth. Walker were first registered with U.K.C. as part of the English Coonhound breed. Then in 1945, at the request of Walker breeders, U.K.C. began registering them as a separate breed—first as Walkers (Treeing) and then later as Treeing Walkers.

This standard was formed and revised for the purpose of guiding Bench Show Judges, Breeders, Breed Participants and Single Registration. The Treeing Walker breed was founded and has become dominant because of its ability to run and tree game, therefore, this recognizes the need for variety and individuality within the breed as terrain and/or other purpose shall demand.

———— ✳ ————

The Treeing Walker was developed from certain strains of English Walker Foxhounds. Credit for developing the American Walker Foxhound goes to two men: George Washington Maupin and John W. Walker, both from Kentucky. Before then, Thomas Walker, of Albemarle County, Virginia, imported hounds from England, beginning in 1742. In 1770, George Washington, an avid foxhunter, also imported several hounds from England. These dogs became the foundation strains of the Virginia hounds, from which the Walker came.

(Photograph of "Texas Lotto" courtesy Tom Culpepper)

GENERAL APPEARANCE

Symmetry, or conformation, is of great importance. Denotes quality. Working dogs will not be penalized, under any conditions, for scars or blemishes due to hunting injuries.

DEFECTS: Poor conformation.

QUALITATIVE CHARACTERISTICS

Energetic, intelligent, active, courteous, composed, confident, fearless, kind, graceful in pose and while active. Super abundance of sense, endurance, trailing, hunting and treeing instinct and ability.

HEAD AND SKULL

The head is carried well up. Occiput bone prominent; cranium broad and full. Head in pleasing proportion to body. The muzzle is medium square, rather long. Slightly tapering, with flews sufficient to give a rather square appearance. Stop not too prominent, not too abrupt.

DEFECTS: A very flat skull, narrow across the top. Excess of dome. Muzzle long and snippy, cut away below eyes too much, or very short. Roman nosed, or upturned, giving a dish-faced expression

TEETH

Should meet; not overshot or undershot.

EYES

Moderately prominent; set well apart. Open, soft and expressive. Dark in color; brown or black.

DEFECTS: Eyes small, sharp and terrier-like; too protruding.

NOSTRILS

Rather large, prominent and black. A slightly sloping nostril not objectionable.

FAULTS: Other colors.

EARS

Of medium length, set moderately low. Should hang gracefully, inside part tipping toward muzzle. Should not be too pointed at tip, but slightly round or oval, soft and velvety, hanging with a tendency to roll when head is raised. In proportion to head and body.

DEFECTS: Ears short, set high or with a tendency to rise above the point of origin.

NECK AND THROAT

Neck rising free and light from the shoulders. Strong in substance, yet not loaded. Of medium length. Throat should be clean and free from folds of skin. A slight wrinkle below the angle of the jaw, however, is allowable.

DEFECTS: A thick, short neck carried on a line with the top of the shoulders. Throat showing dewlaps and fold of skin. Too "throaty."

FOREQUARTERS

Forelegs—Straight, with a fair amount of bone. Pasterns short and straight.

DEFECTS: Out at elbow, Knees knuckled over forward, or bent backward. Forelegs crooked.

BODY

Shoulders sloping, clean, muscular. Not loaded or heavy in appearance. Conveying the ideas of freedom of action, springiness with activity and strength. Chest should be deep for lung space. Look for depth rather than width. Well sprung ribs. Back ribs should extend well back, about a three-inch flank allowing for springiness. Back moderately long, muscular and strong. Loins broad and slightly arched.

DEFECTS: Straight, upright shoulders

Chest—Disproportionately wide, or with lack of depth. Flat ribs. Very long, swayed or roached back. Flat, narrow loins.

HINDQUARTERS

Hips and thighs strong and well muscled, giving abundance of propelling power.

Hind Legs—Stifles strong and well let down. Hocks firm, symmetrical and moderately bent.

DEFECTS: Cowhocks, or straight hocks, Lack of muscle and propelling power.

FEET

Solid, compact, well-padded, giving a cat-like appearance. Well arched toes, strong nails for quick getaway. Close and firm.

DEFECTS: Feet long, open or spreading.

TAIL (STERN)

Set rather high. Strong at root. Tapering, moderately long without flag. Carried free, well up, saber-like. Curved gracefully up and forward.

DEFECTS: Too long, rat tail, entire absence of brush.

COAT

Smooth haired. Glossy, fine, yet dense enough for protection. A close, hard, hound coat.

DEFECTS: Short, thin coat, or of soft quality.

COLOR

Tri-colored is preferred, white-black-tan. White may be the predominant color, with black spots and tan trim; or black may be the predominant color with white markings and tan trim, such as saddle back or blanket back. White with tan spots or white with black spots may be accepted.

DEFECTS: Any other color combination will be penalized when shown.

VOICE

Preferably a clear, ringing, bugle voice; or a steady, clear chop. Noticeable change at tree.

HEIGHT

Slightly more at shoulders than at hips. Shoulders should measure: Males, 22" to 27"; Females, 20" to 25".

WEIGHT

Should be in proportion to dog's height. Working dogs not to be penalized when shown if slightly under.

DISQUALIFICATIONS

Unilateral or bilateral cryptorchid. Extreme viciousness or shyness.

SCALE OF POINTS

Head	10
Neck	5
Shoulders	10
Chest & Ribs	10
Back & Loins	15
Hindquarters	10

Elbows	5
Legs & Feet	20
Coat & Color	5
Stern (Tail)	5
General Make-up	5
Total	100

This breed is recognized by the United Kennel Club, the Continental Kennel Club, the National Kennel Club, and American Pet Registry, Inc.

Notes and Sources

CHAPTER 1. HOWE AND WASHINGTON
JOIN THE ARMY

He did not hang: Abbot, W. W., "The Uncommon Awareness of Self," in *George Washington Reconsidered*, ed. George Higginbotham, Charlottesville: University Press of Virginia, 2001, pp. 110–11.

Best horseman of: Mount Vernon Ladies Association, *George Washington's Mount Vernon: Official Guide Book*, Mount Vernon, Va., 2004, p. 99.

CHAPTER 4. SWEET LIPS GETS WASHINGTON A JOB

Perhaps the most jarring picture: Ellis, Joseph J., *His Excellency*, New York: Knopf, 2004, p. 44.

As they formed: Ward, Christopher, *The War of the Revolution*, 2 vols., New York: Macmillan, 1952.

the most essential duty: Anderson, Troyer, *The Command of the Howe Brothers During the American Revolution*, New York: Oxford University Press, 1936, p. 77.

CHAPTER 5. THE GENTLEMAN'S CODE

I have been convinced: Commager, Henry Steele, and Richard B. Morris, *Spirit of 1776*, Boston: Da Capo, 1995, p. 164. Original edition 1975.

CHAPTER 6. THE BATTLE OF GERMANTOWN

Every intelligence from town: Trussell, John B. B., Jr., *Germantown*, ed. Donald H. Kent and William A. Hunter, Harrisburg: Commonwealth of Pennsylvania, Pennsylvania Historical and Museum Commission, 1974.

CHAPTER 7. GENERAL HOWE'S DOG

to exaggerate the American Achievement: Ellis, p. 104.

CHAPTER 8. THE WAR ENDS

He is as good: *George Washington's Mount Vernon*, p. 99.

frequently raised a fox: Ibid.

He keeps a pack of hounds: Humphreys, David, *The Life of Washington*, ed. Rosemarie Zugarri, Athens: University of Georgia Press, 1999.

Saturday 18th: *The Diaries of George Washington*, vol. IV (1784–June 1786), ed. Donald Jackson and Dorothy Twohig, Charlottesville: University Press of Virginia, 1978, pp. 277–83.

Washington arrived and moved: McCullough, David, *John Adams*, New York: Simon & Schuster, 2001, p. 427.

He stopped by the stable: Willard Stern Randall.

ADDITIONAL SOURCES USED THROUGHOUT THE TEXT

Coren, Stanley. *The Pawprints of History*. New York: Free Press, 2002.

Derr, Mark. *A Dog's History of America*. New York: North Point Press, 2004.

Ellis, Joseph. *His Excellency*. New York: Knopf, 2004.

Fischer, David Hackett. *Washington's Crossing*. Oxford: Oxford University Press, 2004.

Flexner, James Thomas. *Washington: The Indispensable Man*. Boston: Back Bay Books, 1994.

Gruber, Ira D. *The Howe Brothers and the American Revolution*. New York: Norton, 1972.

Kelley, Joseph J., Jr. *Life and Times in Colonial Philadelphia*. Mechanicsburg, Pa. Stackpole Books, 1973.

Lemish, Michael G. *War Dogs*. Washington, D.C.: Brassey's, 1996.

McGuire, Thomas, *The Surprise of Germantown, or the battle of Cliveden, October 4th, 1777*. Gettysburg, Pa.: Thomas Publications and Cliveden of the National Trust, 1994.

Partridge, Bellamy. *Sir Billy Howe*. London: Longmans, Green, 1932.

Randall, Willard Sterne. *George Washington: A Life*. New York: Owl Books, 1994.

Rees, Abraham. *The Cyclopedia or Universal Dictionary of Arts, Sciences, and Literature,* vol. XII. Philadelphia, 1805.

Rowan, Roy, and Brooke Janis. *First Dogs*. Chapel
Hill: Algonquin Books, 1997.

Tunis, Edwin. *The Tavern at the Ferry*. Baltimore:
Johns Hopkins University Press. 2002.

———. *Colonial Living*. Baltimore: Johns Hopkins
University Press. 1999.

Wiencek, Henry. *An Imperfect God*. New York: Farrar,
Straus, Giroux, 2003.

SOURCES FOR
ORIGINAL CORRESPONDENCE AND
OTHER DOCUMENTS

George Washington Papers, Manuscript Division,
Library of Congress, Washington, D.C.

George Washington Papers, University of Virginia.

INTERVIEWS

Bob Gleason, American Historical Theatre, Philadelphia.

Stephen Hague, executive director, Stenton Historic
House Museum, 4601 N. 18th St., Philadelphia.

Thomas McGuire, author, historian, and narrator for
the annual Battle of Germantown Day.

Philip Seitz, curator of History, Cliveden of the National Trust, 6401 Germantown Ave., Philadelphia.

William Sommerfield, artistic director, American Historical Theatre, Philadelphia.

VIDEOS

George Washington: The Man Who Wouldn't Be King, WGBH Educational Foundation, *The American Experience*, 1992.

Acknowledgments

Thanks to Carlo De Vito and to Ron Martirano, the publisher and editor, respectively, of this book, for helping bring it to fruition. I'd also like to thank Josh Freely, who was an unparalled companion for Battle of Germantown Day and who patiently explained to me how a person can be passionate about three-cornered hats and, accordingly, all things Revolutionary. Finally, many thanks to the highly skilled authors, historians, dog aficionados, curators, and reenactors who so generously shared their perspectives and knowledge.